Social Sciences : a second level course
New trends in geography   Units 13–15
prepared by the course team

Political, historical and regional geography

The Open University Press

The Open University Press
Walton Hall, Bletchley, Bucks.

First published 1972

Designed by the Media Development Group of the Open University.

Printed in Great Britain by
EYRE AND SPOTTISWOODE LIMITED
AT GROSVENOR PRESS PORTSMOUTH

SBN 335 01533 6

This text forms part of the correspondence element of an Open University Second Level Course. The complete list of units in the course is given at the end of this text.

For general availability of supporting material referred to in this text, please write to the Director of Marketing, The Open University, Walton Hall, Bletchley, Bucks.

Further information on Open University courses may be obtained from the Admissions Office, The Open University, P.O. Box 48, Bletchley, Bucks.

1.1

Contents

Introduction to Block IV

Introduction to Block IV

Scale in political geography — macro and micro

Into this block are compressed the briefest accounts we could contrive concerning changes in three branches of human geography – political, historical and regional geography. Each one of these could have occupied a whole block – or even a whole course – under different conditions; in this half-course, we thought it best, as you know, to give the lion's share to the substantial developments in theoretical bases and the interface with border disciplines in economic and social geography. Yet in the three fields studied in this block there are some exciting developments to report: historical geography has perhaps never been more dynamic, more ready to complement the historian's approach with its own spatial analyses; much political geography still follows traditional methods, and as a result much good work is done, but it has its own challenging interface with psephology (the study of voting behaviour), as we shall see; much regional geography seems to be poles apart from the new interdisciplinary field of regional science, yet we have thought it worth while to call our third unit in this block 'Regional geography to regional science', and indeed it may be that a renaissance in regional studies is in prospect. So the course team thought we must include some treatment of these fields in the course, however selective we must necessarily be.

We have tried to concentrate on ways in which recent changes in geography as a whole have been reflected in each of the three fields. Inevitably we have often had to choose examples to illustrate the trends in order to attain some depth of treatment, rather than cover the whole of a field in a more superficial way. Even so, parts of each unit include broad surveys of the field; we have tried to avoid mere name-dropping, which we know is frustrating to students working at home and often without access to good libraries, by giving at least a sentence or a phrase to outline something of the approach or aspect of the study undertaken by a particular worker. Even so many readers will be frustrated in some places, and we can only hope that if you cannot read as widely as you would like during the course, you may find an interest within it which you can follow up in later years, perhaps using some entry points into the literature from our text and bibliographies. Success in the course will depend on the main themes set forth, rather than on the detailed byways of our topics however entrancing these are to explore at leisure. Our aims and students' objectives are set out at the beginning of each unit.

Books which will be of use to you in working through the block are:

Set Book

Board, C., Chorley, R. J., Haggett, P. and Stoddart, D. R. (eds.) (1969) *Progress in Geography: International Reviews of Current Research*, Arnold, London. K. R. Cox on 'The voting decision in a spatial context' (pp. 81–117), is relevant to Unit 13. We think most students should read the correspondence unit before attempting to tackle this fairly difficult paper, especially the second part by Dr. Gwyn Rowley. Students have already been referred, in Block I Unit 3 of the course, to P. R. Gould on 'Methodological developments since the fifties' (pp. 1–49). This is a very closely packed review paper, and students will find that they gain more and more from this type of paper as they get deeper into their study of geography. Section IV.2 of Gould's paper is on geographical applications of linear programming models, and many may benefit from looking again at these pages (17–18) after they have read the correspondence text and watched the television programme by Professor Learmonth.

Recommended Book

Dury, G. H. (1963) *The British Isles: a Systematic and Regional Geography* (2nd edn.), Heinemann, London, was recommended for use in Block I Part 1 of the course. It is again referred to in Unit 15.

Note: These two books are relevant and useful, but the three units in this block are all self-contained within the correspondence texts and the supplementary material.

Scale in political geography macro and micro

Unit 13 Andrew Learmonth (part one) Gwyn Rowley (part two)

Unit 13 Contents

Part one

1 Political geography – aims and students' objectives

Aims:

(i) to take the student beyond the point in political geography where Foundation Course students were left in Unit 23; that is to take him towards a theoretical framework in political geography of the more traditional kind. This will mainly be on the broad (macro) scale represented there by the Mackinder paper and discussion, focussing particularly on the unified field theory of S. B. Jones (1954) but including more recent work along comparable lines; (note: for students who have not done the Foundation Course the other theme followed was that of frontiers and boundaries as representing studies on a micro scale, and at the same time presented the views of workers opposed to premature generalization. If you can read Unit 23 of Course D100 you will doubtless pick up these particular threads better, but we think you can follow this unit without doing so).

(ii) to show that micro political geography reflects the current revolution in geography rather more than does macro political geography; the focus is mainly on electoral geography, and the cross-links with other branches of human geography are reasonably strong.

Students' objectives:

After finishing this section of the course the student should be able to:

(i) go beyond Mackinder's 'grand generalizations' and the classifications of frontiers and boundaries of Foundation Course Unit 23, and join in the groping towards a theoretical framework for political geography, traditional or in the newer trends;

(ii) work through an example of the unified field approach of S. B. Jones, as a minimum demonstration of grasp of the search for a theoretical framework in traditional political geography; this may be on any scale, macro, meso or micro, and be drawn from a very wide variety of contexts including the student's own reading and experience, providing the evidence is handled in a scholarly way;

(iii) follow and substantially recreate the arguments about methods of analysing and explaining electoral patterns put forward by workers like Cox (1969) and by Dr Rowley in Section 4 below.

2 Towards a theoretical framework for traditional political geography : the macro scale

2.1 Introduction

Students who have read Unit 23 of the Foundation Course will recall that there is a marked contrast between the two parts of that introduction to political geography. On the one hand there is the broader macro scale of Mackinder's paper on the geographical pivot of history as he saw it in Central Asia, and his later discussion of the 'Heartland' area. On the other hand, there is the more intimate scale of Prescott's treatment of frontiers and boundaries, both in our instructional material and in his recommended book *The Geography of Frontiers and Boundaries*, and then in the paper by J. W. House in the Foundation Course Reader *Understanding Society*. House indeed is explicitly critical about premature generalization, whereas Mackinder, writing sixty years earlier, proposed to match grand generalizations in geography with some of the grander generalizations of history. House pleads that only after many painstaking studies of small areas and problems could large generalizations be attempted. Before leaving traditional political geography for the 'New trends' of our course title, it is important to stress that the more traditional approaches, as in other branches of geography, have had their own striving towards a theoretical framework.

We shall briefly review in turn some of the ideas of three political geographers: R. Hartshorne, J. Gottman, and S. B. Jones, and you will note that the macro scale dominates the discussion.

2.2 Hartshorne and the functional approach in political geography

Hartshorne, a political geographer of distinction, wrote an important assessment of trends in the field in 1950. He found the following streams of research and writing:

(i) Descriptions of countries, more or less explanatory at the level of subjective integration, intended to aid understanding of the state or states under discussion but perhaps unlikely to give a good framework for analytical thinking. The student need not dismiss these studies as necessarily at a low level of discussion. For example, Isaiah Bowman's *The New World* (1921) is a readable, scholarly work on the Europe of the years after the Treaty of Versailles which cannot fail to deepen understanding of the problems of the area in that and later periods. It is mainly a descriptive work, ranging over history and geography, but includes explanatory material using judgement or subjective integration. A comparable survey after the Second World War is W. G. East and A. E. Moodie, *The Changing World* (1956). Works like these perhaps lie between this class and the next.

(ii) The historical approach, aiming to show how a state comes to occupy its present territory. One, less satisfactory group of studies takes the present area, boundaries, etc. of the country under discussion and tries to explain them by apparent correspondences with political or physical features. We do not think that for present purposes you should divert your energies to a study of this group. The physical determinist view that there are such things as 'natural boundaries' of states may have its seductions even for the scholar (much more for the polemicist), but for practical purposes there are no natural boundaries. All political boundaries are drawn by human beings in some way, though to be sure natural features are sometimes associated with easily identified points or thinly peopled belts convenient for boundary delimitation (see Foundation Course Unit 23 pp. 15–17).

Then there is a second, more satisfactory group of studies in depth, using documents with all a historian's care as well as field methods if the study is modern, but orientated more to areal organization and cartographic method than are most historical or political studies. In this category Hartshorne himself confesses to a paper in 1950 on the Franco-German boundary of 1871 and suggests also Whittlesey's study of Andorra of 1934 and the same author's 'The Earth and The State' of 1939. House's paper in the Reader *Understanding Society* is an excellent example going beyond the physical appearance of the border areas studied, to their impact on the life of the local people.

(iii) The morphological approach, that is the description and analysis of the shape, size, space-relations etc. of a given political area, that is taking the territory as the core of areal analysis, the core study, in which geographers might be expected to find common ground. This is an approach which Hartshorne himself had suggested as long ago as 1935. But by 1950 he had come to regard this as too static, too dull and in application too often sterile of really significant findings. Some assessment of this approach may be gained from Isaiah Bowman's review article of 1927 concerning some of the current literature, mainly German.

Hartshorne in his 1950 paper therefore goes on to suggest the state, often the focus of national sentiment as a nation-state, as a core area of political geography without, of course, excluding studies of other scales of approaches. The study of the state he pleaded, should be functional, or simply concerned with the state as a functioning unit. Particular aspects of the study might include centripetal or centralizing tendencies including national sentiment, as against centrifugal or decentralizing tendencies including regionalism in its stricter, political sense of more or less separatist tendencies. Centripetal and centrifugal tendencies should be studied as they affect the functioning of the state, including its external relations, but emphasizing the areal or spatial aspects.

You may care to try out the four approaches reviewed by Hartshorne, in barest outline, in relation to some area you know. The United Kingdom may be too large and complex for a simple self-test in your own notebook, but since many students will have considered Northern Ireland in relation to Unit 2 of the Foundation Course, it might be interesting to use it here without, of course, engaging in fresh reading. The approaches are:

(i)   an explanatory description of the area as we now observe it;
(ii)   a study in historical-political geography (a) from a physical-determinist point of view, and (b) by using all sources of evidence;
(iii)   the morphological approach as described above; and
(iv)   Hartshorne's functional approach, as described above.

At the reconnaissance or quick-assemblage level of assessment, which do you find the most satisfying?

2.3   Gottmann on iconography and *circulation*

In a paper in 1951 and a book in 1952 Jean Gottmann suggested that two useful approaches to political geography are to study political units through their iconography, on the one hand, literally their images, their symbols, including national or for that matter regional sentiment, and on the other hand through their *circulation*. The French word *circulation* is best translated into English as embracing circulation of all kinds in a society, movements of ideas as well as goods and people, communication as well as communications. These simple concepts have proved fertile, almost prophetic. The idea of iconography leads to the studies of perception – here the idea that the image of a state is the way in which its inhabitants (or those of a neighbouring state) perceive it, and so can be studied by various devices borrowed from psychology. And the idea of the significance of communications of all kinds has been developed in many studies, such as those in electoral geography discussed later: it is in this way that studies in political geography have become more dynamic and may be developing much more explanation of causes.

2.4   Jones and the unified field theory of political geography

The two basically simple contributions by Hartshorne and Gottmann were among the foundations for further thinking in a paper by S. B. Jones in 1954, on a unified field theory as an approach to political geography. His framework is also extremely simple, though the detailed working out in a full scale case study can be extremely complex. Jones simply suggests that a chain lies between (political) idea and (political) state or situation – here the geographer is likely to focus on political area as the end of the chain: political idea – political decision – political movement – political field – political area.

Jones thinks of his chain as a series of interconnected basins or lakes rather than an iron chain of separate links. To interpolate, these basins might be visualized as connected reservoir basins in a complex hydro-electric and irrigation project assuming though that the flow along connecting channels may on occasion be reversed. Towards the left-hand side of the chain as presented above, the headings belong more to political science, and towards the right, more to political geography. But Jones pleads that it is necessary for the political geographer to understand the left-hand side before he can give a causal analysis relating to the more geographical right-hand side of his flow diagram. If the political scientists provide him with data in the form of digested material in books or articles in the learned journals, so much the better. If not, the geographer may have to do the job himself. In fact, he may have to acquire some of the skills of the political scientist if he is to be an effective political geographer. This problem is often met in geographical work generally, and if you become seriously interested in geography you may find that a particular research problem leads you to delve more deeply into a sister discipline than you had envisaged. It is partly with this in mind that we have started with an inter-disciplinary Foundation Course, and offer some further opportunities to gain a trained competence in sister disciplines in later courses.

One example sometimes used by political geographers in expounding the idea of the unified field theory is the progress from an idea to a nation-state in relation to modern Israel. For a brief treatment see H. de Blij (1967) a recommended text for the Foundation Course.

A first application of the five-fold chain is easy enough, though our political scientist colleagues warn us against a simplistic or unduly simple approach, and indeed we have already noted that the detailed working out of a full-scale study would be highly complex. Jones would plead that to understand the political geography of Israel and the Middle East, a student must follow through the five links. In this particular problem we can start for simplicity's sake with the era of Zionism which belonged to the early twentieth century. Jews including rich and influential ones in various parts of the world were spreading the idea that Jews ought to be able to return to a national home from their very scattered locations all over the world. Obviously, modern Zionism has its own continuing influence, but we can omit this from consideration at this stage.

The second link in the chain, political decision, is here represented by the Balfour Declaration of 1917. This was just a letter from Lord Balfour, then Foreign Secretary, to Lord Rothschild, a prominent Zionist, very briefly stating in principle the British Government's general support for the idea of a Jewish national state. The dangers of over-simplification are apparent. Many earlier events must have conditioned this decision, and looking ahead there were to be many 'ifs' and 'buts'. The war was still to be won; many formalities had to be completed in relation to the defeated Turks and Arab allies in the struggle, irreconcileables reconciled. But the crucial decision, on one reading, lay here in the Balfour Declaration. Again later decisions affecting the whole complex are clear enough, but may be disregarded in a first exercise – for instance, the end of the British Mandate in 1948 after bitter strife between Jewish guerillas and the mandatory power, or again, the six-day war of 1967 and all the subsequent geopolitical tug-of-war. The politically significant movement or movements in the third link, include all the types of movement of Jews towards Palestine (later Israel), the legal and illegal immigrants under the Mandate, and the many post-war movements of refugees and of

Jews drawn to return to the national home. Many subsequent politically significant movements in the sense of movements of troops, naval units, air power, rocket power and so on would clearly be involved in the complex skein of a full-scale study, but again may be disregarded in a first exercise in the approach. The movement of Arab refugees from Israel is clearly also part of the current picture which takes us beyond the present political boundaries of Israel. This leads us to the wider political area involved which merely focuses on Palestine or Israel. For some purposes we should need to complement our study by a wider study, embracing at least the Middle East as a whole.

This becomes very clear in turning to the fourth link, the political field. The term 'field' here is used partly by analogy with fields of force or of potential in the physical sciences, like a magnetic field or field of gravity. These are only analogies and like all analogies should not be over-strained. Jones distinguishes between kinetic fields and dynamic fields. Kinetic fields are those which involve movements which are accepted by both sides and which one might characterize as productive movements or productive exchanges across a political boundary. Dynamic fields on the other hand, involve movement or exchange across political boundaries which arouse conflict. To change our area of reference, the flow of raw jute from Bangladesh (East Pakistan) to West Bengal is mainly kinetic, the flow of refugees was mainly dynamic. As we know the political field around Israel remains only too active and dynamic in Jones's sense. It is here that we should clearly have to broaden the area of study if it is to be meaningful. We should have to take account of the Arab refugees in adjacent countries and their emotional effect on the various host countries and on the Arab world as a whole. We should have to take account of the Palestinian Arab movement which refuses even to use the word Israel, and includes the guerilla and sabotage element which has caused loss of civil aircraft of international airlines. Then there is the Pan-Arab movement which at one time appeared likely to produce a truly United Arab Republic of power and cohesion embracing most of the Arab world. There is the involvement of the two super-powers, USSR and USA, in this area of conflict. And there is the particular reason for the eastern and western powers alike to have a strong economic and strategic interest in the Middle East because of its importance in relation to world supplies and especially reserves of petroleum.

You may have gained some understanding from following Jones's chain of lakes and linking channels. The approach is sometimes a useful one though clearly not the only one. It does not belong particularly to political geography, but expressed in the way we have tried to outline it does culminate on the right-hand side of the original set of concepts, in political fields and political area which do belong particularly to political geography.

So far as we know the unified field theory has not been successfully translated into a mathematical model or manipulated in a quantitative way, though this may have been done behind the locked doors of defence or external affairs departments. However, you may care to try a (voluntary and optional) exercise to see if Jones's approach seems to take you further in understanding than you had attained by normal reading and reasoning as a citizen:

(i)   Start near the centre of a large piece of paper, say roughly two feet by two feet (or stick several pieces of your normal workpaper together). Draw a sketch-map of Israel just above the centre, a sketch-map of the Middle East just below.

(ii)   Use the top left-hand corner for annotations on the map about political ideas, Zionism in the early twentieth century, Zionism in its continuing impacts and so on.

(iii)   Use the centre of the top of the paper for annotations following through from political ideas to political decisions: the Balfour Declaration, the British Mandate, the Six-day War, and so on.

(iv)   Use the top right-hand side of the paper for annotations on the map dealing with political movements, the movements of Jewish patriots, idealists and intellectuals, or of refugees and people of various kinds of occupations, education and culture from a wide variety of countries; the movement of funds and aid from the USA and other countries.

(v)   Use the bottom right for annotations on the map about the political field as explained above.

(vi)   On the bottom left annotate the sketch maps in relation to the characteristics of the political area, of the political frontiers or area of intermingling and interdigitation of differing groups, of the political boundaries, stable or mobile, delimited, demarcated and so on.

Then try an assessment. Probably the circumstances are unique – there is only one Israel. All the same, can generalizations be made, about decolonization, about the survival of a small nation apparently surrounded by enemies? Or does the method lead only to dangerous over-simplification? Should one risk over-simplification at a certain stage in order to attain some understanding of the general picture and the general movements involved, even if one then wants to qualify this over-simplified approach by putting back carefully selected detail which one has discarded in an effort to follow through the five stages of the unified field theory?

Additional sources

Some students may find it helpful to start from Pounds, N. J. G. and Kingsbury, R. S. (1966) *An Atlas of Middle Eastern Affairs*, London, Methuen. Many libraries hold Keesing's Contemporary Archives, a valuable summary of the news.

Part two

3 Electoral geography : a progress report on studies mainly on the micro scale

3.1 Introduction

Consideration of the upper echelons within the political hierarchy, as typified by the nation state, morphological descriptions of political areas and environmental-political relationships, have been a constant preoccupation within political geography. This concentration towards the macro or regional level has tended to impede the development of theory and sets of related hypotheses within political geography, defined here as *the spatial analysis of political phenomena*, and place much of political geography together with regional geography outside the mainstream of changes that have increasingly characterized geography in the last two decades. From Mackinder's time British political geographers have especially studied nation building and expansion; recent examples include Cole's study (1959) of the geographical factors behind world affairs and Prescott's studies (1965, 1968) of political frontiers and of nation states.

Electoral geography, itself an integral part of political geography, is concerned with the geographical analysis of elections at the various levels of government in federal and unitary states (Prescott, 1969, 1972). The viewpoint adopted here is that electoral geography represents an interface between political geography on the one hand and social geography on the other. The approach has some claims to synthesize other approaches: to what extent is voting behaviour explained by economic analyses? (Buchanan and Tullock, 1961), or again by those of the sociologist? (Easton, 1957.)

There were early classic studies of the spatial analysis of voting behaviour like Krebheil's work on British elections (Krebheil, 1916); but despite this, electoral geography has only recently re-emerged as a research interest within the United Kingdom. By contrast, in France a continuing series of studies have associated voting behaviour with population characteristics and socio-economic status, like Siegfried's (1947) regional study of voting in the Ardèche area and Goguel's work on national elections (1951 and 1961). Kasperson (1969) has shown that electoral studies have long been a dominant focus of research in American political geography, where geographers have concentrated upon the temporal and spatial variations of voting aggregates (or blocks of votes), and their association with environmental, social and economic variables. In Britain, however, both teaching and research within political geography remained relatively unimportant after the halcyon days of Mackinder. This is possibly linked to the decline of Great Britain as a world power and the previous very particular interests of both British political scientists and British political science journals. This contrasts with the breadth normally exhibited by their North American and Continental counterparts. Indeed, within Britain the re-emergence of an interest in electoral geography has stemmed largely from a prime interest in a behaviourist approach to human geography rather than an interest in the political system as such. Again, there was until quite recently, little fundamental research on the British electorate apart from the notable contributions of Nuffield College, Oxford, to psephology (the scientific study of elections), for example the work of D. E. Butler (1966).

17

The three aspects of elections that have been of recurrent interest to geographers are first, the study of the geographical factors behind electoral patterns. Secondly, geographers have been interested in the way that governments are often sensitive to electoral patterns and seek to alter the economic geography of certain constituencies and territory, for example, to increase government popularity. Thirdly, geographers have sought to comprehend the geographic reasons, if any, that lead to the adoption of the particular electoral method employed, together with the selection of boundaries within a chosen scheme (Prescott, 1969).

3.2 Recent developments

Recent developments within electoral geography as in geography as a whole have not only been characterized by increasing empiricism but also by a real concern for theory. Burton, for example, has inferred that geography became scientific when its methodology adopted a theoretical framework (Burton, 1963). Presently, however, more subtle innovations are underway within geography, steadily gaining in momentum, especially since the mid 1950s. Four characteristics define these changes that have occurred and are occurring: (i) the interdependence of quantitative and theorizing activity is most apparent; (ii) the revolution in scientific technology is appreciated and utilized for further work; (iii) the behaviour of the individual is taken as the basic unit of analysis; (iv) the recognition that research techniques and findings of other disciplines have both relevance and applicability to geographical research (Eulau, 1963).

The development of a quantitative-theoretical orientation together with

Figure 1
Elements in the Funnel of Causality

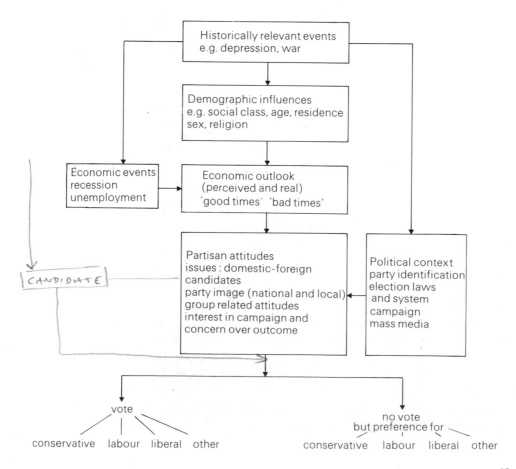

associated technical innovations in geography is relatively well documented. These trends, it should be emphasized, do not represent complete reorientation within existing methodology but rather the superimposition of further themes that in time have become increasingly dominant.

Geography however, is not unique in these developments: other social sciences have also placed increasing emphasis on behavioural analysis. Nonetheless, the behaviour of the individual is increasingly being adopted as the basic unit of analysis and this represents a reaction to generalized geographical data that tended to disregard the underlying behavioural reality (Olsson and Gale, 1968). Problems have to be faced. The behaviourist is a super-disciplinary being, unhampered by the modes of one subject area or, conversely plagued by the idiosyncracies of all. Thus if geographers are to become active in common research areas at the interdisciplinary level they must, of necessity, become conversant with existing literature – not only geographical literature in the narrow sense, but all that is pertinent to their field of inquiry.

3.3 The behavioural context of electoral geography

Although no general theory of voting behaviour exists, the funnel of causality, developed at the Survey Research Centre (SRC) of the University of Michigan, provides a framework for vital analyses: firstly, why certain people vote and others do not; and secondly, how people choose one party or candidate rather than another (Campbell *et al.*, 1960).

The funnel represents a comprehensive and orderly theoretical scheme to describe how a variety of influences mould and modify political opinion,

Figure 2
Influence process in the Funnel of Causality

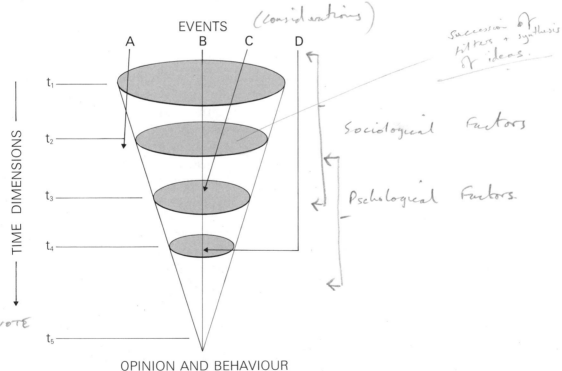

OPINION AND BEHAVIOUR

participation and behaviour (Figure 1). The SRC believes that an individual's political attitudes and behaviour result from the convergence of a number of independent variables that may be classified as (i) historical, (ii) institutional, (iii) sociological, and (iv) psychological.

Figure 2 indicates how a variety of events may influence an individual's

19

field of political perception, the sloping sides of the funnel representing the limits of this perception field. At Time 1 events A, B, and C are personal and politically relevant, while at Time 2 event A has now become irrelevant. Events B and C are both politically relevant but combine at Time 3 into a single force that effects both opinions and behaviour at Time 5. Event D, previously an external factor, has become personal and politically relevant at Time 4, and represents a second influence upon opinion and behaviour at Time 5.

The steps entailed in operationalizing these items pose problems for behavioural research. Broadly, however, we may concur with Pulzer when, referring particularly to Britain he asserts that 'sociology in the main explains the reasons for long term (party) loyalty; psychology is more useful in explaining why some people change' (Pulzer, 1967). Studies in the geography of party preference and electoral participation have thus, in Britain, tended to stress the relationships between socio-economic characteristics and electoral behaviour and their variation over space (Cox, 1968; Roberts and Rummage, 1965).

3.4 Data problems

The very real problems associated with data sources, and the comparability between sources, have also retarded the development of electoral geography within Britain. Lacking the rich, inviting and accessible resources afforded by, for example, the SRC and a number of heavily financed integrated inter-departmental investigations in electoral behaviour undertaken in the USA, together with the creation of related data banks, researchers working within a British context have to use material of dubious value. By contrast, for example, at the SRC voting behaviour research has been able to focus increasingly upon the voter rather than the vote by means of continuing series of national sample surveys.

Again, whereas census tracts and electoral divisions are broadly comparable in the USA, discrepancies often occur between British data sources. For example, Prescott (1969) notes that it is singularly unfortunate that Roberts and Rummage (1965), and Cox (1968) in two recent studies of the spatial variation of electoral behaviour in British urban areas, do not explain how they match censal and electoral information. What is more, the limitations of aggregate data present another difficulty (Ranney, 1962). Only constituency data are available and no breakdown even to the level of the polling station is possible. Kahan, Butler and Stokes (1966) further question the accepted boundary between the 'middle' and 'working' classes and note that research into the political effects of class is peculiarly dependent on the manner in which classes are defined empirically. In spite of these problems we will present two studies in electoral geography that indicate, at two quite different scales, work in progress.

3.5 Regional considerations

Firstly, we present a report of a research project now in progress, concerning long term population change and its effect upon the British electorate. Simple classification and tabulation of results of the General Elections of 1964 and 1966 reinforces the notion of an often observed traditional dichotomy which differentiates the Conservative dominated lowland Britain, apart from London and the urban and mining settlements of the Midlands, from the Labour dominated Highland Britain, excepting national variations in Northern Ireland (not mapped), the Scottish Highlands and the Southern Uplands.

Figure 3
The distribution of party control after the General Election of 1966

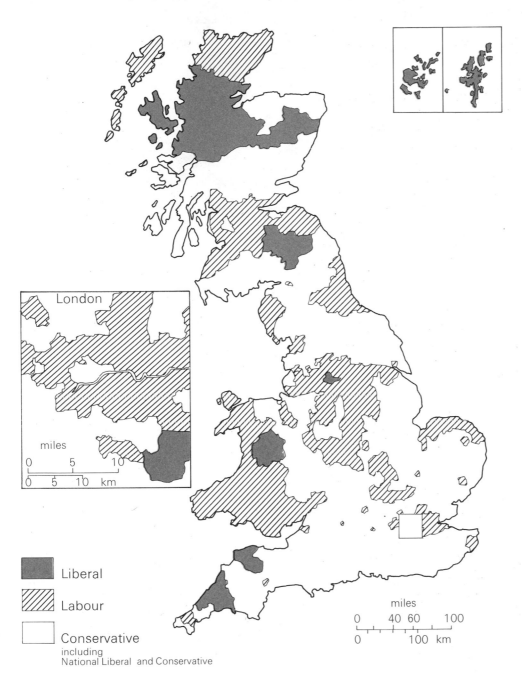

A major problem emerges when it is realized that the Labour constituencies are heavily concentrated within regions with declining populations. An inference would thus suggest an erosion of the traditional Labour strongholds if these population trends continue.

3.5.1. Party majorities and electorate change

An analysis of the relationship between party majorities and electorate change was undertaken for a 20 per cent sample (19·56 per cent) of English constituencies in the 1966 General Election (Rowley, 1970). Forty-seven Labour and 43 Conservative constituencies were sampled and scatter diagrams constructed of the percentage majority the winning party obtained over the second party, and the percentage change in the electorate between 1959 and 1966 (Figures 4 and 5).

Figure 4
Percentage electorate change 1959–66 and the percentage majority the winning party attained over the second party for a 20 per cent sample of English constituencies returning a Conservative member at the 1966 General Election

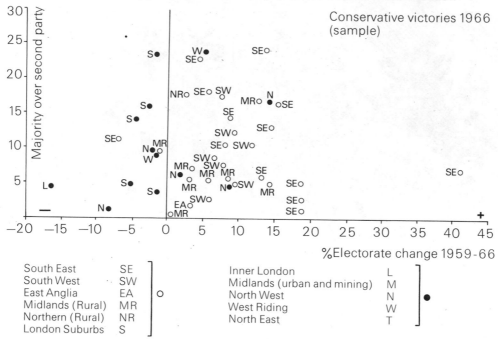

South East	SE		Inner London	L
South West	SW		Midlands (urban and mining)	M
East Anglia	EA	o	North West	N
Midlands (Rural)	MR		West Riding	W
Northern (Rural)	NR		North East	T
London Suburbs	S			

Figure 5
Percentage electorate change 1959–66 and the percentage majority the winning party attained over the second party for a 20 per cent sample of English constituencies returning a Labour member at the 1966 General Election

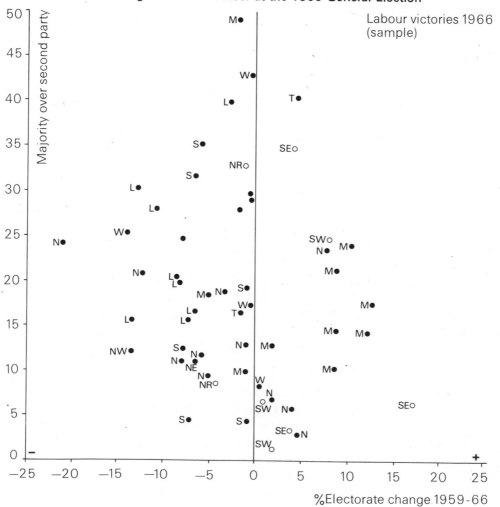

Using the 20 per cent sample data four analyses were undertaken using simple χ^2 tests.[1]

Hypothesis	Confirmed/Rejected
1 That the percentage Conservative majority and the percentage electoral change 1959–66 were independent (not related)	Confirmed at 95 per cent significance level, so population decline does not seem to affect Conservative held constituencies by increasing or decreasing majorities over next party
2 The result in 1 was tested further by a measure of association, which turned out low (0·01)	Lack of association confirmed
3 That among Conservative-held constituencies with declining populations there was no relationship between larger decline and larger majorities	Confirmed, so the conclusion under 1 above is strengthened
4 That the proportion of Labour-constituencies with declining populations did not differ from the proportion of Conservative-majority constituencies with declining populations	Rejected, so Labour-constituencies probably are associated with declining populations

On the basis of these findings all English constituencies returning a Labour member at the 1966 General Election were considered (Figure 6). Of the 285 Labour constituencies 189 (66·32 per cent), or almost exactly two-thirds,

Figure 6
Percentage electorate change 1959–66 and the percentage majority the winning party attained over the second party for all English constituencies returning a Labour member at the 1966 General Election

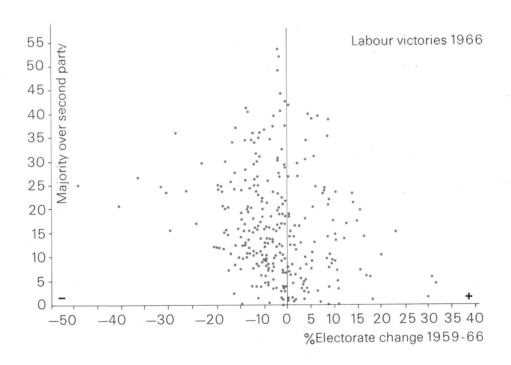

1   The χ^2 test is a simple and very valuable method of testing a hypothesis. It can often be used where the numbers can be tabulated for (a) observed data (b) expected values, that is, expected according to hypothesis. This is done by setting up a null hypothesis, that is, that there is no significant difference between observed data and expected values. If this null hypothesis is assessed as not true at a given level of probability, 19 to 1, or 99 to 1, or 999 to 1, then with increasing confidence the original hypothesis can be accepted as proved. These levels are often referred to as in the following text as the 5 per cent, 1 per cent or 0·1 per cent significance level. These are the complementary figures – there is only a 5 per cent (1 in 20), a 1 per cent (1 in 100), or a 0·1 per cent (1 in 1000) chance that the hypothesis is not proved, that the null hypothesis maintains. You will note from the following paragraph that the test can also be used to establish the independence of two variables. You will find details of the technique in Gregory 1968 (a prescribed text) or almost any elementary text on statistics, if you are interested.

experienced declines within their electorates between 1959 and 1966. What is more, 76 per cent of the Labour constituencies in England possessing a declining electorate between 1959 and 1966 had a Labour majority of over 10 per cent in 1966. Conversely, 64·6 per cent of Labour constituencies with an increasing electorate between 1959 and 1966 had a majority of less than 15 per cent. Again a startling contrast is that two-thirds of Conservative constituencies in 1966 had increasing electorates.

The simple inference from the preceding remarks is that the traditional Labour strongholds are declining.[1]

3.5.2.   The Greater London Council elections

As opposed to the national scale, we may discern important variations in the electoral geography within the large conurbations and cities. Here we shall consider one such conurbation, Greater London, which contains more than one-fifth of the total electorate of the United Kingdom, as revealed in the results of the 1964 and 1967 council elections.

The spatial pattern of political representation resulting from the Greater London Council election of 1964 (Figure 7) and analysis of variations in the size of both majorities and 'swings' between political parties as compared with the 1959 elections prompted speculation as to the existence of a concentric zonal model of electoral behaviour – a central zone of conservative boroughs (Westminster, Kensington and Chelsea), an inner ring of Labour areas composed of Safe Labour and Marginal Labour boroughs, and a peripheral zone of Conservative boroughs (Rowley, 1965).

Although the peripheral ring of Conservative boroughs was broken at Hillingdon and Hounslow in the west and at Havering and Bexley in the east, a consideration of the results of the 1964 election within these boroughs indicates that the Labour majorities were quite marginal (Figure 8) and a small swing of the order of 4 per cent from Labour to Conservative would probably have completed this concentric zone. This pattern of political behaviour was, briefly, related to the social areas of the Greater London conurbation as defined in the report of the 1951 census (Figure 9). Comparisons with the theories of urban structure, such as those of Burgess and Hoyt also suggest themselves here (Social Science Foundation Course Team (1970) *Understanding Society*, Course D100 Unit 21).

Thus on the basis of the results of the Greater London Council elections of 1964, a theory relating to the spatial variation of political behaviour was formulated. A later study sought, firstly, to test the hypothesis suggested previously relating to the regularity of the pattern of political behaviour on the basis of the Greater London Council elections of both 1964 and 1967; secondly, to develop techniques for the investigation; and thirdly, to consider the conclusions, relating the findings to the existing theory, determining the implications of the findings for the theory, and comparing these findings with previous observations. In this short account party majorities will be considered, whereas the full research report also included an appraisal of both electoral swing and turnout.

---

1   Beyond the scope of a quantitative study in electoral geography such findings may be linked with matters of broader concern. To the extent that areas of declining population are also Development Areas, these findings may throw light on the contention that past Labour Government interest in and assistance to the Development Areas contrasts with Conservative intentions, at least at the time of writing of the paper cited, to abolish the Regional Employment Premium in September 1974 (Chapman, 1970). Of course the redrawing of electoral boundaries and reallocations of Parliamentary seats consequential upon population changes is also a topic linked with studies like that just discussed in the text.

Figure 7
Representation on the Greater London Council 1964—Distribution of party

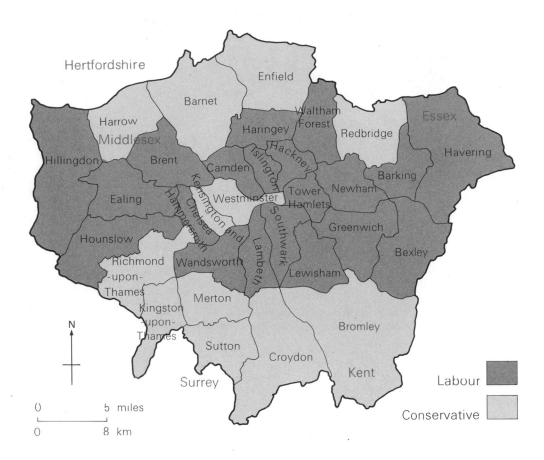

Figure 8
Dispersion diagrams of average majorities, 1964 and 1967

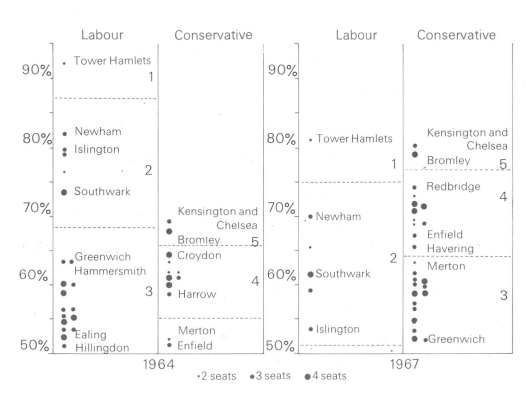

Figure 9
Social areas of the Greater London Conurbation 1951

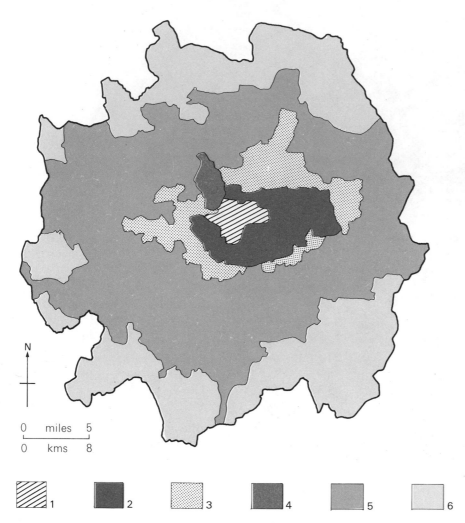

N

0   miles   5
0   kms   8

☐1   ■2   ☐3   ■4   ■5   ☐6

1   Metropolitan commercial and administrative centre
2   High density old residential, industrial and dockside areas
3   Hampstead type
4   Newer residential and industrial suburban districts
5   Outer rural
6   residential fringe

3.5.3. The election of 1967

Primary consideration of the results of the 1967 election utilized both carto-graphical and graphical methods of analysis. The map of the distribution of party control in 1967 (Figure 10) shows the location of the six boroughs returning Labour representatives, together with Greenwich, which returned two Conservatives and one Labour councillor. This latter result, it must be emphasized, is not an example of 'split ticket' voting as encountered with the USA, but rather an indication of the extreme marginality of Greenwich in 1967.

Dispersion diagrams of average majorities were constructed to facilitate further analysis and understanding of the results (Figure 8). The varying sizes of the proportional circles used in the dispersion graphs represent the number of seats, varying from two to four, elected by constituents within a borough. A Greater London Council seat is related to approximately 50,000 electors. Thus, a borough with 100,000 electors, or thereabouts, returns two councillors, whereas a borough with approximately 200,000 electors returns four council members. Data for the graph have been derived by computation from the election returns for each borough. Briefly, the average number of votes obtained by all Labour and all Conservative candidates within the borough was ascertained, this being followed by a study of the percentage majority the average Conservative total obtained over the average Labour total, or vice versa. For example, in 1967 the Labour candidates for the two seats in Barking received 14,444 and 12,591 votes. By contrast the Conservative candidates received 7,646 and 6,732 votes. This represented an average vote to Labour and Conservative of 13,512 and 7,189 respectively, while the Labour average vote was 65.3 per cent of the average Labour plus Conservative vote cast in Barking in 1967.

In only one borough, Bromley, where Conservatives won the seats in 1967, did the Labour party fail to take second place as a party, in this instance running third to Liberal. Similarly in 1964 the Conservative party failed to take second place in only two boroughs where Labour gained the seats, again owing to Liberal intervention.

The dispersion graphs of average majority may be used as a basis for a classification of boroughs. The method by which each group is defined and recognized derives from the contention that group members relate more with other group members than they relate to non-group members, that is, within-group distance or variance is minimized and, by definition, between-group variance maximized. The observed discontinuities in both 1964 and 1967 are denoted by broken horizontal lines and the groupings numbered for later identification. Five classes may be differentiated on the basis of size of majority in both the election of 1964 and 1967. These are (1) Very Safe Labour, (2) Safe Labour, (3) the Marginals, (4) Safe Conservative, (5) Very Safe

Figure 10
Distribution of party control 1967

N

| 0 | miles | 5 |
| 0 | kms | 8 |

Labour

Conservative

Split vote

two Conservative and
one Labour returned
(Greenwich)

Conservative. It should be emphasized that the third group in 1964 includes Enfield and Merton. The fortunes of the Conservatives were at a low ebb in 1964 but, with a swing of 13·4 per cent from Labour to Conservative between the results of 1964 and 1967, they achieved a dominant position in the latter election. In electoral terms this resulted in the Conservatives gaining control of the Greater London Council in 1967 with 82 seats as opposed to only 18 held by Labour, a Conservative majority of 64. In contrast in 1964, Labour had been successful in returning 64 councillors and the Conservatives only 26.

In detail the arithmetic mean of the swing from Labour to Conservative within the 32 boroughs between the elections of 1964 and 1967 was 13·37 per cent, with a standard deviation of 5·29 per cent. Swing is here defined as the average of one party's gain and another party's loss. An analogy may be drawn between the dispersion diagram and a U-tube or manometer, perhaps most familiar to many of us from the instrument used in medical examinations to measure blood pressure. A manometer is an instrument for measuring differences in pressure, where ordinarily the weight of a column of liquid is balanced against the pressure to be measured. Likewise the dispersion diagram shows a similarly related adjustment between parties, an upswing in the Conservative column being matched by a commensurate change or decline in the Labour column between the two elections. The analogy enables us to understand the most significant group of electoral swings, the twenty-two observations, 0·69 or slightly more than two-thirds of the boroughs, included between the two ordinates that are located one standard deviation on either side of the mean.[1] The number of boroughs between one of two standard deviations away is 7 or 0·218. Together these two groups constitute a little over 90 per cent of the observations, and all the results fall within three standard deviations of the mean.

To facilitate the appraisal of the dispersion diagram of average majorities, histograms of the frequency distribution of classes in both 1964 and 1967 were constructed. The graphs (Figure 11) describe the class frequency of members; generalized curves are also included. The frequency curve, constructed on the basis of the numbers of seats in each class, approximates to the normal distribution, although slight skewness is evident in both elections. Skewness is here defined as the lack of symmetry in the shape of the frequency curve. This, on the basis of these two elections, illustrates the larger number of ostensibly Safe and Very Safe Conservative seats.

In detail few changes of class membership occurred between the two elections. Later analysis of swings between the parties revealed that a certain change is projected through the system with scarcely any deviation from the average (Rowley, 1971). However, despite the utility of the dispersion graphs (Figure 8)

---

1 The standard deviation is a measure of the variability of the values in a group of statistical values being studied. It is used for many statistical manipulations, but one vital function it performs well is to *complement* the arithmetic average (a valuable expression of the central value of a group of figures which yet may conceal within similar averages the very different ways in which they are derived; a mean annual rainfall of 25 in. may result from annual totals consistently around 25 in., or from alterations between drought years of 10 in. and wet years with 40 in.). The standard deviation is calculated by taking the difference between each value and the arithmetic average, squaring it, totalling all these differences, dividing by the number of values being studied, and finally taking the square root of that answer. A common shorthand prose description is the root mean square deviation, or in formula form:

$$\sigma = \sqrt{\frac{(x - \bar{x})^2}{n}}$$

where σ (sigma) is the standard deviation, x is each successive value, $\bar{x}$ is the arithmetic average, and n the number of values being studied.

and histograms (Figure 11) in facilitating description, it was deemed necessary to undertake a more refined method of analysis of changes between the two elections.

The fundamental hypothesis suggested is that those changes which occurred between the results of 1964 and 1967 have spread equally through the system and the basic observed spatial variation remains constant. That is, the relative differences between the various boroughs, for example, Tower Hamlets, Greenwich and Merton, in the election of 1964 and 1967, are approximately

Figure 11
Histograms of the results of the 1964 and 1967 elections

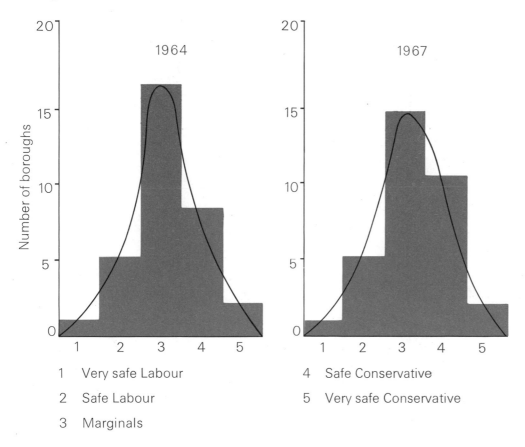

1   Very safe Labour   4   Safe Conservative

2   Safe Labour   5   Very safe Conservative

3   Marginals

maintained despite the swing against Labour. Swing is here defined as 'the average of one party's gain and another's loss' (Leonard, 1968). This analysis of association between the two elections may be developed by utilizing a rank-order correlation coefficient. As coefficients of rank areal association are non-parametric they require no assumptions about the nature of the population distributions (Neft, 1966). It should also be recognized that the observations may be treated as possessing the characteristics of a population but not those of a sample.

The Spearman rank-order correlation coefficient, which is dependent upon the possibility of ranking both variables, is used in this analysis.[1] The dispersion diagram of average majorities facilitates this procedure, the data being ranked according to their positions within the dispersion graph of 1967 and 1964 (Figure 8). For example, in 1967 the ordering is Tower Hamlets (1), Newham (2), . . . Islington (6), Greenwich (7) . . . Bromley (31), and Kensington and Chelsea (32).

---

1 Students of the Foundation Course *Understanding Society* may have come across the use of this coefficient in connection with a psychology exercise.

Table 1
Boroughs by rank order in 1967

Borough (ranked by 1967 order)	Percentage of vote obtained by successful party		Difference in rank	
	1967	1964	D_i	$D_i{}^2$
1 Tower Hamlets	81·1*	92·4*	0	0
2 Newham	69·9*	82·1*	0	0
3 Barking	65·3*	76·4*	+2	4
4 Southwark	61·4*	73·4*	+2	4
5 Hackney	58·8*	79·3*	−1	1
6 Islington	53·4*	79·6*	−3	9
7 Greenwich	52·6	63·6*	0	0
8 Lewisham	52·9	60·2*	+1	1
9 Camden	53·5	56·3*	+3	9
10 Wandsworth	54·6	58·5*	+1	1
11 Hounslow	56·4	55·5*	+3	9
12 Haringey	56·7	56·2	+1	1
13 Brent	58·6	54·8*	+2	9
14 Lambeth	58·7	55·1*	+1	1
15 Waltham Forest	59·6	60·2*	−5	25
16 Harrow	59·6	58·7	+7	49
17 Ealing	60·0	53·1*	+2	4
18 Bexley	60·2	54·1*	−1	1
19 Hammersmith	61·4	63·5*	−11	121
20 Merton	63·2	51·7	+2	4
21 Havering	65·4	54·1*	−3	9
22 Enfield	67·2	51·2	−1	1
23 Hillingdon	68·7	51·3*	−3	9
24 Richmond upon Thames	68·7	63·5	+5	25
25 Sutton	69·4	61·5	+2	4
26 Croydon	70·8	64·0	+4	16
27 Westminster	71·3	61·1	−2	4
28 Barnet	71·6	60·5	−4	16
29 Kingston upon Thames	73·0	61·6	−1	1
30 Redbridge	74·2	61·2	−4	16
31 Bromley	78·9	67·5	0	0
32 Kensington and Chelsea	80·0	68·9	0	0
			$\Sigma D_i = 0$	$\Sigma D_i{}^2 = 354$

   * denotes Labour majority
  + indicates a higher rank in 1967
  − indicates a lower rank in 1967
  Σ means the sum of

The ranking within Table 1 is therefore based upon the percentage of the vote obtained by the successful party. Stated somewhat differently and adhering to a common ranking scale deriving from Labour's percentage of the vote, Greenwich (7) would be 47·4 per cent and Kensington and Chelsea (32) would be 20·0 per cent. Reference to the dispersion diagrams of average majorities (Figure 8) will aid comprehension. Of course, no change in ranking results from either of these methods of presentation.

Comparison of the observed rankings by the Spearman rank correlation demonstrates the manner in which the two variables (the results of 1967 and 1964) correlate in ranking (Note 1). By computation a rank correlation coefficient of $r = 0.93$ is obtained. Since the magnitude of r is high, the association between the two rankings is high.

The analysis may be further developed by testing whether the votes for Labour by borough in 1964 and 1967 are related, employing a product-moment correlation and using the original observations as opposed to the rankings used in the Spearman test.[1] The product-moment correlation measures the dependence between two series, in this instance the votes for Labour by borough in 1964 as opposed to 1967. As the value of this correlation coefficient is 0.91 the vote for Labour by borough in 1964 and 1967 may be said to be highly correlated. It is therefore concluded that these are not independent sequences but are very much dependent upon each other, that is, while changes have occurred in political representation between 1964 and 1967, this apparently represents a systematic change throughout the boroughs, with only relatively insignificant deviations from the average change. Further, this implies a verification of the earlier theoretical conjectures concerning an observed regularity within the pattern of electoral behaviour in Greater London (Rowley, 1965). It should, however, be emphasized that correlation analysis cannot be directly used to infer causality, as correlations merely measure covariance.

3.6 Conclusions

This section represents an introduction to electoral geography and deals with two examples from continuing studies concerning the spatial regularities in, and variation of electoral behaviour and relationships with other factors, especially socio-economic ones. It is suggested that whereas Cox (1969) attempts to relate the voting decision of individuals to their location in an information flow network it is perhaps also important to study residential location, its relationship to residential search behaviour (Wolpert, 1965) and residential grouping and segregation and then relate this back to voting behaviour.

The Greater London study and the national study provide results that not only further our insights of reality in studying certain socio-geographical relationships, but also poses important practical applications. Examples of such uses are: first, as a guide for the more effective differentiation of electoral units. Secondly, since redistribution of constituency boundaries within the United Kingdom recur every 15 years while the more mobile population of the last third of the twentieth century is tending to produce more rapid numerical distortions of the electorate, projection of population changes would provide a more realistic definition of threshold values for constituencies for the whole of a 15-year period. For example, it is interesting to note that each of the Safe Labour boroughs in Greater London experienced a population decline between 1961 and 1971. Thirdly, such studies facilitate the more mundane yet important operations associated with political campaigning. To conclude, it is envisaged that electoral geography will continue to develop especially through the analysis of survey data that will facilitate behavioural study of the individual voter, thereby further strengthening the bond between political and social geography.

Note

The difference between any pair of variables is symbolized as D_i and N is the number of individuals ranked. We may therefore compute the value of ΣD_i^2

---

1 Interested students will find an account of the product-moment correlation technique in Gregory (1968) pp. 187–200.

and compute the Spearman's rank correlation coefficient, known as Spearman's r_s measure, by means of the formula:

$$r_s = 1 - \frac{6 \ \Sigma D_i^2}{N \ (N^2 - 1)}$$

We obtain the following by substituting our computed observations into the formula thus:

$$r_s = 1 - \frac{6 \ (354)}{32 \ (1023)} = 1 - 0 \cdot 074 = 0 \cdot 926$$

If the rankings agreed perfectly ΣD_i^2 would be zero and the value of r_s would be unity. Hence a rank correlation of $0 \cdot 926$ is very high.

References

BUTLER, D. E. (1966) *The Study of Political Behaviour*, London, Hutchinson.

BURTON, I. (1963) 'The Quantitative Revolution and Theoretical Geography', *The Canadian Geographer*, Vol. 7, p. 160.

BUCHANAN, J. and TULLOCK, G. (1962) *The Calculus of Consent*, Michigan, Ann Arbor.

DE BLIJ, H. (1967) *Systematic Political Geography*, New York, John Wiley. For a brief extract from this book on 'The Heartland Debate' see our Reader *Understanding Society* (1970) pp. 409–13, London, Macmillan.

BOWMAN, I. (1922) *The New World*, New York, World Book Company.

BOWMAN, I. (1927) *Geographical Review*, Vol. 17, review article p. 511–12.

COLE, J. P. (1959) *The Geography of World Affairs*, London, Penguin.

CAMPBELL, A. *et al.* (eds.) (1960) *The American Voter*, pp. 18–37, New York, John Wiley.

CHAPMAN, K. (1970) 'Conservative policies for the regions', *Area*, Vol. 3, pp. 8–13.

COX, K. R. (1968) 'Suburbia and voting in the London Metropolitan area' *Annals of the Association of American Geographers*, Vol. 58, pp. 111–27.

COX, K. R. (1969) 'The voting decision in a spatial context', in Board, C., Chorley, R. J., Haggett, P. and Stoddart, D. (eds.) *Progress in Geography: International Reviews of Current Research*, Vol. 1., London, Edward Arnold.

EAST, W. G. (1965) *The Geography Behind History*, London, Nelson.

EAST, W. G. and MOODIE, A. E. (1956) *The Changing World*, London, Harrap.

EASTON, D. (1957) 'An Approach to the Analysis of Political Systems', *World Politics*, Vol. 9, pp. 383–400, and in the D100 Reader *Understanding Society*, pp. 491–501, London, Macmillan/Open University Press.

EULAU, H. (1963) *The Behavioural Persuasion in Politics*, New York, Random House.

FISHER, C. A. (1968) *Essays in Political Geography*, London, Methuen.

GOGUEL, F. (1951) *Géographie des élections françaises de 1890 à 1951*, Paris, Colin.

GOGUEL, F. (1961) 'Géographie du refèrendum de 8 janvier 1961', *Revue française de science politique*, Vol. 11, pp. 5–28.

GOTTMANN, J. (1951) 'Geography and International Relations', *World Politics*, Vol. 3.

GOTTMANN, J. (1952) *La Politique des Etats et leur Géographie*, Paris, Colin.

HARTSHORNE, R. (1950) 'The Franco-German Boundary of 1871', *World Politics*, Vol. 2, pp. 209–50.

HARTSHORNE, R. (1935) 'Recent Developments in Political Geography', *American Political Science Revue*, Vol. 29, pp. 511–12.

HARTSHORNE, R. (1950) 'The Functional Approach in Political Geography', *Annals of the Association of American Geographers*, Vol. 40, pp. 95–130.

HOUSE, J. W. (1968) 'A Local Perspective on Boundaries and the Frontier Zone: two examples from the European Economic Community', in Fisher, C. A. (ed.), *Essays in Political Geography*, pp. 327–44, London, Methuen.

JONES, S. B. (1954) 'A Unified Field Theory of Political Geography', *Annals of the Association of American Geographers*, Vol. 44, pp. 111–23.

KAHAN, M., BUTLER, D. and STOKES, D. (1966) 'On the analytical division of social class', *British Journal of Sociology*, Vol. 17, pp. 122–33.

KASPERSON, R. (1969) 'On suburbia and voting behaviour', *Annals of the Association of American Geographers*, Vol. 59, pp. 405–11.

KREBHEIL, E. (1916) 'Geographic influences in British elections', *The Geographical Review*, Vol. 6, pp. 419–32.

LEONARD, R. L. (1968) *Elections in Britain*, p. 24, London, van Nostrand.

MACKINDER, H. J. (1919) *Democratic Ideals and Reality*, London, Constable.

MACKINDER, H. J. (1904) 'The Geographical Pivot of History', *Geographical Journal*, pp. 421–44, reprinted in the D100 Reader *Understanding Society*. pp. 396–409, London, Macmillan.

NEFT, D. S. (1966) *Statistical analysis for areal distributions*, Regional Science Research Institute, Philadelphia, pp. 129–30.

OLSSON, G., and GALE, S. (1968) 'Spatial Theory and Human Behavior', *Papers and Proceedings of the Regional Science Association*, Vol. 21, pp. 229–42.

PRESCOTT, J. R. V. (1965) *The Geography of Frontiers and Boundaries*, London, Hutchinson.

PRESCOTT, J. R. V. (1968) *The Geography of State Policies*, London, Hutchinson.

PRESCOTT, J. R. V. (1969) 'Electoral studies in political geography', in Kasperson, R. E. and Minghi, J. V. (eds.) *The Structure of Political Geography*, Chicago, Aldine.

PRESCOTT, J. R. V. (1972) *Political Geography*, London, Methuen. (Chapter 4 on electoral geography is simply written, tending to favour traditional approaches, but is rather allusive.)

POUNDS, N. J. G. and KINGSBURY, R. S. (1966) *An Atlas of Middle Eastern Affairs*, London, Methuen.

PULZER, P. (1967) *Political Representation and Elections: Parties and Voting in Great Britain*, p. 113, London, Allen and Unwin.

RANNEY, A. (1962) *Essays on the Behavioural Study of Politics*, Urbana, University of Illinois.

ROBERTS, M. C. and RUMMAGE, K. W. (1965) 'The Spatial Variation in Urban left wing voting in England and Wales in 1951', *Annals of the Association of American Geographers*, Vol. 55, pp. 161–78.

ROWLEY, G. (1965) 'The Greater London Council Elections of 1964: some geographical considerations', *Tijdschrift voor Economische en Sociale Geografie*, Vol. 56, pp. 113–4.

ROWLEY, G. (1970) 'Elections and Population Changes', *Area*, Vol. 3, pp. 13–18.

ROWLEY, G. (1971) 'The Greater London Council elections of 1964 and 1967: A study in electoral geography', *Transactions of the Institute of British Geographers*, Vol. 53, pp. 117–31.

SIEGFRIED, A. (1947) *Géographie électorale de l'Ardèche*, Paris, Colin.

SIMON, H. (1957) *Models of Man*, pp. 204–5 and p. 196, New York, Wiley.

SOCIAL SCIENCE FOUNDATION COURSE TEAM, (1970) *Understanding Society*, Unit 23, London, Macmillan.

WOLPERT, J. (1965) 'Behavioural aspects of the decision to migrate', *Papers and Proceedings of the Regional Science Association*, Vol. 15, pp. 159–69.

WHITTLESEY, D. (1934) 'Andorra's Autonomy', *Journal of Modern History*, Vol. 6, pp. 147–55.

WHITTLESEY, D. (1939) *The Earth and the State: a study in Political Geography*, New York, Holt.

Acknowledgements

Grateful acknowledgement is made to the following for figures used in this unit:

Institute of British Geographers for Fig. 2 in *Area*, 1, 1970, Figs. 4, 5 and 6 in *Area*, 3, 1970, Figs. 7, 8, 9, 10 and 11 in *Transactions*, 53, 1971.

Has
historical geography
changed ?

Unit 14 Dennis Mills

Unit 14   Contents

The Open University gratefully acknowledges that Section 1 of this unit is based largely on Chapters 1 and 5 of A. R. H. Baker (ed.) *Progress in historical geography*, David and Charles, Newton Abbott, 1972.

Has historical geography changed?

1   The 'new' and 'old' methodologies

1.1   Aims[1]

Historical geography shares with mainstream geography all the major debates about techniques and methodology and the nature of the subject; but it also has its own special problems arising out of its concern with the time dimension. In this part of the course, therefore, the reader is familiarized with the relationship of historical geography to the discipline as a whole, with some of the materials, methods and results of research in historical geography and with some of the changes in approach noted during the last quarter century.

In Section 1 we present a concise introduction to the methodology of historical geography, which, of necessity, comes close to an oversimplification of the issues involved. However, a few brief examples of scholarly writing in this field are given and references are cited to appropriate, easily accessible works. Section 2 introduces settlement studies in historical geography and a consideration of a static model of nineteenth century villages comes in Section 3. The associated telecast deals with a dynamic model of industrial and urban growth in the United States, and in the radio programme there is a discussion of the relationships between sociology, geography and history.

1.2   Continuity and change

It was made clear at the beginning of this course that both continuity and change have been evident in geography since the last world war. The New has not completely replaced the Old. The need for continued attention to empirical, so-called descriptive work, is especially notable in historical geography, which attempts to encompass a wide range of pre-historic and historical periods. It also has to contend with peculiar problems of data collection connected with retrospective investigations and the difficulties of comparing different sets of data amassed for different contemporary purposes. Side by side with empirical work, the last decade has seen the emergence of new approaches depending rather more on rigorous statistical analysis, a greater concern for the behavioural environment and the formulation of general propositions for testing in different regions and in different periods. In particular, there is a new concern with the old problem of historical geography, namely how to deal with the time dimension.

Historical geography has, nevertheless, lagged behind mainstream geography in its response to the theoretical revolution. One reason must be the personal inclinations of the relatively few specialist historical geographers, many of them with first degrees taken in Arts faculties, notably in conjunction with history. As change is now overtaking history, especially economic history, it is reasonable to expect historical geography to feel the influence of this change.

The data of historical geography do not always lend themselves to the latest statistical techniques. Hence, change based on the introduction of new techniques, an important element of change in mainstream geography, has been relatively weak in historical geography. A third possible reason for

---

1   Before reading this correspondence text, Open University students may find it helpful to look at the Reading Notes on Unit 14 in the supplementary material.

relatively slow change is that theory rests on current criteria of rationality. Theory to be applied to historical data needs to be constructed in terms of the context of the appropriate period of time being studied.

1.3   Time and space

We have already seen how history and geography differ from all other sciences (Block 1, Part 2, pages 42–3). While biology and politics, for instance, concern themselves with more or less discrete bodies of fact, the uniqueness of history and geography lies in the dimensions of time and space, within which they study a range of phenomena, in principle unrestricted by any other boundaries. Geography has set itself the task of explaining inter-related spatial patterns. How can this endeavour be carried on simultaneously with a similar exercise in the time dimension? Hartshorne (1959, pp. 103–4) put the problem this way:

> If we imagine a series of air photographs taken of a single area in England, and from the same point in the air, on a mid-summer day every year during the past twenty centuries, and viewed as a motion picture film by geographers and historians, the historians would quite possibly consider it a historical picture, but certainly geographers would call it geographic. Each would see different things in the same picture. To the geographer, this would be a presentation of areal variation as it changed through time; if every individual photograph is geographic, surely the series as a whole is geographic.
>
> Unquestionably, the problem of analysing such a composite of variations through both space and time would be extremely complex. To emphasize the practical difficulty, however, cannot prove an impossibility; it is a warning that if any useful results are to be obtained, the ambitious student must seek ways of reducing some of the difficulties to the minimum.

One of the common ways of reducing the difficulties has been the use of the cross-sectional approach, in both historical and present day geography, for the present is merely the most recent of an unending series of cross sections. A cross section may be defined as the geography of a country or region at a particular point in time, i.e. an historical cross section. By concentrating on a series of static patterns, the student eliminates, for the time being, the problem of studying historical change. His cross section is historical geography mainly in the sense that it is not present day geography.

While, however, a student may collect a series of static patterns, in the form of maps and photographs, any explanation of these patterns is bound to go beyond an examination of the factors operating at that time. Here we have both the dilemma and the great opportunity of the historical geographer. On the one hand, too great a concern with the time dimension leads him back into the field of history, yet on the other hand, he wishes to give due prominence to the principle of geographical inertia.

Geographical inertia is a reference to the fact that spatial patterns often remain relatively unchanged long after the causative forces·which led to their establishment have declined considerably in importance. New causative forces, such as technological change, must be radical and powerful if they are to overcome this inertia. Such a change is now being experienced in agriculture, especially in arable farming, with the effect that miles of hedgerows are being uprooted so that modern machinery can be used to best advantage. Hitherto the hedgerow has been a most durable feature of the landscape and has even survived in many built-up areas as a property division. Another excellent example of geographical inertia has already been studied in this course, namely the Durham pit villages described by Andrew Blowers in Unit 12.

Historical momentum is an alternative phrase indicating a complementary notion to geographical inertia, e.g. old established cities in the USA, simply by being established, possessed an initial advantage in gathering momentum during the period of industrial expansion in the second half of the nineteenth century (Pred, 1966).

Before passing on, it may be helpful to look briefly at one further opportunity for the principle of geographical inertia that occurs in *Understanding Society*, p. 351:

> A striking curiosity of the concentric model [of zoning in cities] might seem to be the fact that poor families live close to the urban centre on high-value land while the rich live at the city edge where land is cheaper.

The explanation suggested for this apparent anomaly is based on the lower cost of *present* journeys to work in the central business and manufacturing district; but one might equally consider the quite different scale of land values in operation *at the time when* the low grade housing was erected in the nineteenth century. In some cities the pressure for land use change in the inner residential zone has not reached a point where it can overcome the inertia which is working to keep the use as it is; in other cities, this inertia has been reinforced by the social policy of housing authorities, who have replaced the old housing with new working class accommodation. (Figure 1.)

1.4   The 'old' framework of historical geography

In a newly published book, Baker (1972) describes the traditional framework of historical geography in terms of three approaches: cross section; vertical theme (or vertical development); and the historical element in geography. On

Figure 1
Illustrating cross sections, vertical themes and the historical element in geography
Example: Imagine a historic British city with a cathedral and clerical quarter.
This would develop rapidly in the early middle ages and then suffer a slow
relative and absolute decline as a feature of the urban landscape

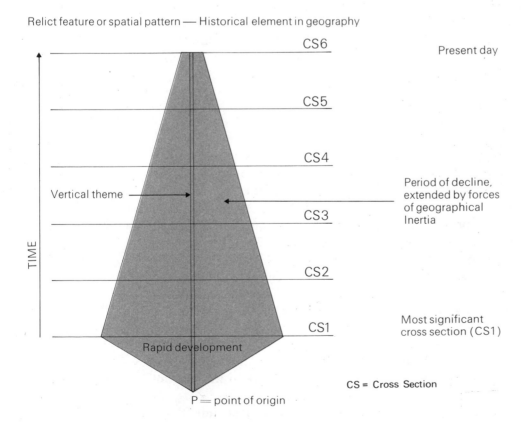

occasion, individual studies have been presented almost entirely in terms of only one dimension, but a combination of two and often all three dimensions has been the more usual. For example, the enquiry may have been prompted by some unresolved problem in present-day geography, which sent the worker back into the historical element. Having found the significant cross section (for his purpose), he might then link it up to the present day by means of a vertical theme of evolution or development.

1.4.1 Cross sections

The use of historical cross sections has been very widespread, not only because it provides a secure geographical or spatial framework in the form of a static picture, but also because in many instances the historical geographer finds himself confined to important non-recurring sources of information. The *Domesday Geographies*, edited by H. C. Darby's team, are a classic instance of this kind, but there are plenty of other examples, such as studies of the crop returns of 1801 and Felkin's census of stocking frames taken in 1844.

However, as we have already seen, a cross-sectional approach cannot be self-sufficient, when it comes to seeking causes (see 1.3). Furthermore, a complete cross-sectional picture can seldom be made up for a narrowly defined point in time. For example, the 1801 crop returns omitted information on stock and although they were collected in the same year as the first British census, this coincidence did not extend to many other important fields of activity. Therefore, it is impossible to write a regional agricultural geography of Britain in the year 1801, in the literal sense, and the cross section, in practice, has often become a period picture.

Historical geographers using the cross-sectional technique to reconstruct past geographies have often been caught up in the mainstream debate between the environmental determinists and the possibilists. During the decades when it seemed that the geographer's main task was to relate human activity to the physical environment, historical geographers concentrated much of their effort on cross-sectional studies of *landscapes* (for example, Balchin 1954, Harris 1961, and Millward 1955, who wrote on the making of the English landscape; Harris is discussed briefly below).

1.4.2 Vertical themes

These are themes in which the changes in spatial patterns of, say, an industry or a railway network, are followed through from the period of earliest development to the present day. Of the three major types of the 'old' historical geography, the vertical theme has most closely resembled history, sharing with it the narrative form of presentation. Harris's book on the East Riding is significant in that it demonstrates one of the older ways of combining cross sections with vertical development. Thus, a discussion of 'The old order' (the rural landscape of the early eighteenth century) is followed by 'Changing countrysides, 1730–1810'. This use of the vertical development approach comes by way of explaining 'The new order', or the rural landscape in the 1850s. Thus two cross sections are joined up by a single piece of vertical development. This approach was first used on a large scale by Broek (1932): in his book on the Santa Clara valley, four cross sections are linked by three intervening chapters on the social and economic forces at work in that part of California over time.

The vertical development approach has also been used independently of cross sections. A number of good examples can be found in Mitchell (1954), a typical instance being the account of the changing geography of the iron industry, from which the following paragraph is taken (p. 255):

> Four major periods preceding the present may be distinguished. In the first, from earliest times to the early eighteenth century, ore was smelted, until about 1500 on a bloomery hearth, later in a blast furnace, and refined in forges, using charcoal as fuel at all stages in the manufacture. . . . This was the Age of Charcoal. In the second period, roughly coincident with the middle decades of the eighteenth century, iron was smelted with coke fuel in the blast furnaces but was refined in forges still using charcoal fuel. . . . This was the age of transition. In the third period, in the late eighteenth and first half of the nineteenth century, with the introduction of the steam engine and of the puddling process by which iron could be forged with coke, the industry was freed from dependence on water for power and wood for fuel. . . . This was the age of coal. In the fourth period, the late nineteenth century, the demands of the markets for steel and the limitations of the first cheap steel-making processes gave a great incentive to iron industries with easy access to non-phosphoric ores. . . .

This account is then expanded for the next 28 pages, in which a detailed analysis of locational factors and a description of the industry's geographical distribution are given for each of the four periods, on a more or less chronological basis.

1.4.3   Historical element in geography

Perhaps we could define the historical element in geography as those spatial patterns of present-day geography that were established in former historical periods, when economic, technological and other circumstances were significantly different. The following three criteria will help to make clearer the distinction between vertical development and the historical element:

(i)   In vertical development the geographer works towards the present day, whereas the opposite is often the key characteristic in analyses of the historical element in geography. He may, for example, set himself the task of dating all the features in the landscape he is studying.

(ii)   When the historical element is a prominent feature of the geographer's work he frequently starts from the recognition of relict landscape features or spatial patterns, leading to

(iii)   The genesis or origin of these features or patterns.

Good examples of an overriding concern for origins may be found in the chapters in Darby (1936) which deal with the Anglo-Saxon and Scandinavian settlement of England and in Ward's study of the pre-urban cadaster of Leeds, where street patterns are related to field boundaries of the pre-industrial period (Baker *et al.*, 1970).

The study of relict features in the landscape has received longstanding support from the emphasis placed on fieldwork by historical geographers. Prince's article on the *origin* of pits and depressions (1964) not surprisingly starts off:

> So much of Norfolk is flat and ploughed down to bare earth that it is easy to pick out slight irregularities and declivities on its surface; but until recently neither historians nor naturalists have studied in detail many thousands of small hollows, to be seen in almost every field in central Norfolk. (p. 15.)
> The form of the pits and depressions suggests the possibility of four different modes of origin: that they are old, abandoned mineral workings; that they are former marl pits; that they are formed by the solution of underlying calcareous material; that they are periglacial features formed by the thawing

Figure 2
Density of pits in Norfolk

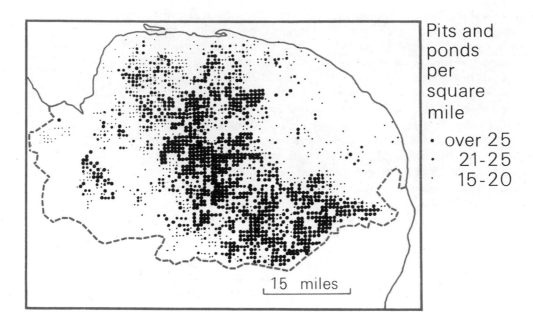

Pits and
ponds
per
square
mile

• over 25
• 21-25
 15-20

15 miles

of ice embedded below the surface. The location of over 27,000 steep-sided pits marked on current Ordnance Survey maps serves as a framework for assessing the relative merits of the four hypotheses. (p. 17.) (Figure 2.)

Thus we see within a mainly traditional study the introduction of the idea of hypothesis testing.

1.5 The 'new' framework of historical geography

Even within the 'old' framework, the historical geographer already had many choices open to him. Apart from the three approaches of the old framework, he might veer towards or away from environmental determinism, he might emphasize landscape features or embrace spatial patterns, such as those relating to place names and religious beliefs, which were not directly observable in the landscape. Sometimes the nature of the source material set constraints, at other times it encouraged, on pragmatic grounds, the branching out into new avenues of enquiry. Notice in this connection that Prince's material gave him the opportunity to construct a grid distribution map, a mildly quantitative approach to his problem.

Out of a variety of methodological changes, Baker (1972) sets before us the emergence of a new threefold framework, consisting of the real, perceived and theoretical geographies. Reference to 'real' historical geography has at least two implications: firstly, the need to continue with investigations in some of the older traditions, at least partly in order to increase the body of historical material, processed from a geographical point of view, against which theoretical propositions may be tested. Secondly, the term 'real' is used to mark the distinction between the phenomenal environment (i.e. an environment consisting of tangible, real objects) and the behavioural or perceived environment. The distinction has been present for a long time, but the rise of the behavioural sciences must have drawn attention to it, making geographers think about it more consciously. The first geographer to draw out this latent interest and sharpen its cutting edge was Kirk (1951 and 1963). Although this is a development historical geography shares with mainstream geography, the study of the behavioural environment is especially pertinent to it, as Kirk has shown in his 1963 paper.

1.5.1   The behavioural environment

The core of Kirk's argument runs as follows:

> We have been led by an over-emphasis on material objects of study to consider man and environment as things apart, and consequently have been drawn into discussions of environmental determinism and possibilism which spring from this dichotomy, but our real responsibilities remain within the unified field of the Geographical Environment and the problems it generates. Within this field the true division of geographical labour is not between man and environment but between Phenomenal Environment (including the works of man) and Behavioural Environment as is suggested in Figure 3. (p. 364.)
> The same empirical data may arrange itself into different patterns and have different meanings to people of different cultures, or at different stages in the history of a particular culture, just as a landscape may differ in the eyes of different observers. . . . [The Behavioural Environment] is the environment in which rational human behaviour begins and decisions are taken which may or may not be translated into overt action in the Phenomenal Environment.
> . . . Facts which exist in the Phenomenal Environment but do not enter the Behavioural Environment of a society have no relevance to rational, spatial behaviour and consequently do not enter into the problems of the Geographical Environment. (p. 366.)

To illustrate Kirk's point, the location of the British coalfields was of no geographical relevance before coal came into use. This is a warning not to look at the industrial historical geography of this country with a mind conditioned by the behavioural environment arising out of Victorian coal-based industries: the earlier quotation from Mitchell illustrates the impact of changing technology upon environmental perception and locational behaviour patterns. As Kirk remarks, 'Historical geographers and western geographers interpreting oriental landscapes are particularly exposed to such pitfalls' (p. 368).

We have already seen some instances of ideas that fall readily into Kirk's framework. Both Broek and Harris paid considerable attention to 'Socio-economic processes and changing environmental values', while Prince was concerned with features of the phenomenal environment, some of which were 'physical relics of human action', some the results of 'inorganic processes and products'.

An increasing interest in the behavioural environment, manifested in mainstream geography by, for example, studies in decision-making, has particular relevance in any cross-cultural studies. By definition, historical

Figure 3

geography is an exercise in cross-cultural thinking, as even the historical geography of one's own country involves an effort to think in terms of the behavioural environment of former stages in the development of its culture. This strand of geographical thinking receives some attention in the two later sections of this unit.

1.5.2 Statistical methods

A less well-rooted trend is that towards a greater use of statistical data and more rigorous analysis of already well-known statistical information: in one word, quantification. The roots are shallower partly because much of the historical geographer's information does not readily lend itself to this kind of treatment. One common problem concerns the fact that surviving data do not always comprise representative samples; for instance, in the historical geography of eighteenth-century agriculture estate records over-represent the large tenant farms and tell us very little about small owner-occupied farms.

In one respect, however, the effort to quantify is a continuation of a well-established habit in historical geography, namely the testing of the validity of source material, an activity which has received much support from historians having parallel interests. Such is the importance of documentary information that in their series on historical geography, David and Charles have published

Figure 4
Cereal crops in Herefordshire, 1801

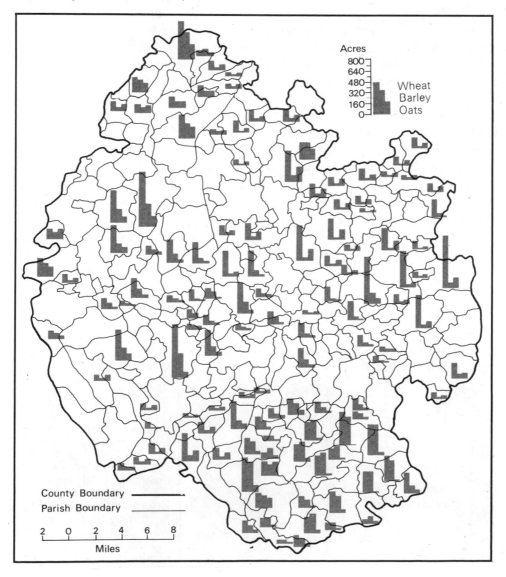

first a book entitled *Geographical Interpretations of Historical Sources* (Baker *et al.*, 1970). This book is a collection of papers demonstrating geographical interpretations of such documents as crop returns, tithe awards, taxation returns and archaeological evidence. The co-operation of geographers and historians in joint projects is admirably illustrated by the Cambridge Group for the History of Population and Social Structure (see, for example Wrigley, 1966). Here also we have an instance of influence coming into both history and geography from the social sciences and of the use of a computer to analyse millions of entries of baptisms, burials and marriages in about 500 English parish registers.

Serious study of the crop returns of 1801 for England and Wales began soon after the last war and Figure 4 is typical of the maps produced from them at this time. A desire for more sophisticated analyses of the same data can be seen in the later work of Thomas (1959). He drew not only four separate maps showing the distribution of wheat, barley, oats, and turnips and rape (a fodder crop) in the Welsh borderland, but also went on to plot the first, second and third ranking crops in this area (Figure 5). The final result was a map of crop combination regions (Figure 6), bringing together a series of complex variables into one spatial pattern. In later work still (Thomas, 1967) regression analysis was used to examine the influence of climatic and distance variables on the production of crops in Wales in 1801.

Perry, again, analysed the distances between the homes of brides and bridegrooms in nineteenth-century rural Dorset, using the sophisticated technique of step-wise multiple regression analysis (Perry, 1969). Put simply, this means that he was able to isolate the relative importance of eight different factors: the population size of the parish, its location (whether a chalk or vale location), apparent literacy of the population married, distance to the nearest railway station, number of other parishes within three miles and the distance from the nearest town, these six factors being probably significant at 90 per cent probability level. The remaining two factors, the pattern of settlement and distance from the nearest main road, proved to be not statistically significant. Although studies of marriage distances go as far back as Peel (1942) and Constant (1948), Perry's greater use of statistical techniques, of which we have seen only a glimpse here, have brought much greater understanding of this aspect of human behaviour. In passing, also notice that the work of Peel and Constant on behavioural problems considerably pre-dated the general application of geographical analysis to this field.

1.5.3   Theory in historical geography and the problem of change through time

Theory, however, does not depend absolutely on quantification: it is a search for the law-responsive, in which quantification is sometimes a most important tool. Although this search for theory has been much intensified during the last ten years, it is not entirely new, as this extract from Mitchell (1954) shows:

> [The value of the historical geographer's works, as a geographer] lies, on the one hand, in the fact that some elements of geographical design that develop in response to passing conditions are extremely stable in their form or long lasting in their effects, and the understanding of the present demands the study of the geography of the period of their establishment and development. On the other hand there is also value in the fact that other elements are rapidly changing and the study of their change and evolution may throw light *on general principles* that determine their geographical pattern . . . (p. 14, our italics.)

So we are confronted once more by the two-fold prospect for historical

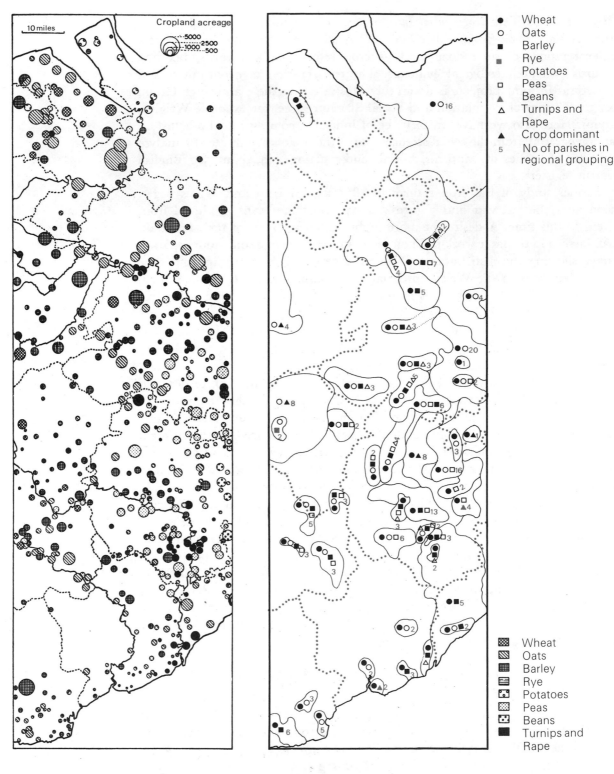

Figure 5
1801 Acreage returns for the
Welsh borderland
Third-ranking crops

Figure 6
1801 Acreage returns for the
Welsh borderland
Crop combination regions

geography: it can follow mainstream geography in developing theories relating to relatively static patterns, but it has a special responsibility in developing theories related to the dynamic aspects of the subject. In response to this challenge, historical geography is beginning, like history itself, to rely less on the narrative approach and more upon measurements of change and models grounded in theory. The contribution of Pred (1966) is examined in a telecast; students may also wish to look at Brookfield's second article in the Reader

Figure 7
The links between London's growth and the Industrial Revolution in England

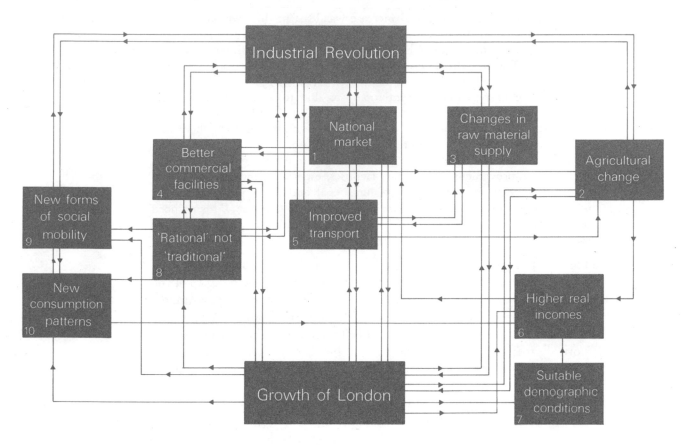

Understanding Society; here we have space to look at the work of two British historical geographers.

Wrigley (1967) has constructed a simple model to elucidate London's importance in the period 1650–1750. It is impossible to make a full comment on Figure 7, but a few basic points will bring out its methodological significance. First, it draws attention to the possibility that we have overlooked the fact that London may have been a motive force of prime importance in the early years of the industrial revolution. Secondly, we should appreciate how the arrows have been drawn to indicate a complex set of interrelationships between the different factors shown in the boxes:

> Many of the changes are connected with the growth of London in two directions, at once produced or emphasized by London's growth and serving in turn to reinforce the growth process, a typical positive feedback situation, to borrow a term from communication engineering. In some cases growth was possible only because of this mutual relationship. For example, the growth of London could not have gone very far if it had not produced substantial change in agriculture over large areas and brought about sufficient improvements in the transport system to make it feasible to maintain a reliable and moderately cheap movement of food surpluses from the home counties and East Anglia into London. In other cases there is no return connection between London and one of the aspects of social and economic change promoted by its growth. For example, the continued growth of London had much to do with the slightness of population growth over the country as a whole, but it would be difficult to argue that the reverse was also true. And in still other cases, even though no arrow is drawn in on the diagram, it is obvious that some degree of connection must have existed. (p. 68.)

In his study of the agricultural revolution in south Lincolnshire, Grigg (1962) constructed maps showing the percentage change in rent per acre, during the periods 1815–43 and 1843–60. This enabled him to measure geographical change and thus to explain it:

> Over the period as a whole rental increase was least in the two clay regions, where rent had been relatively high in 1815; and highest in the Heath and north-west Kesteven, where it had been low in 1815; and intermediate in the Fenland. The net effect was to reduce the regional contrasts in rent per acre, but by no means to eliminate them. (p. 101.)
>
> The decline in regional differentiation was due to a number of factors. First of all the spread of improved farming methods had reduced the farmer's dependence on the natural fertility of his soils. Secondly, in 1815 there had been a marked regional specialization in both land use and the type of product. But between 1815 and 1860 the spread of mixed farming had reduced this. . . . Finally the improvement of transport facilities, especially towards the end of the period, cheapened the import of lime, coal and other producer goods, and facilitated the movement of farm products out of the area. This reduced the differences in accessibility which had influenced rents locally at the beginning of the century. (p. 102.)

While their subject matter and their approaches to it differ, Wrigley and Grigg have in common a determination to study *change* and also an avoidance of the narrative form of presentation. Earlier generations of historical geographers were perhaps so conscious of the need to establish the distinctiveness of geography as a discipline that they guarded their flanks by concentrating on landscapes and historical cross sections. Now that the rudiments of geography are secure, we can confidently reach out to a wider range of spatial patterns and study change for its own sake.

Moreover, we live now in a period of rapid change and as historians are said to rewrite history each generation according to the lights of their time, perhaps the same will become true of historical geographers. In this case it will be true of geographers generally, for we are told that:

> A study of *process* therefore, is not the prerogative of the historical geographer alone. It concerns us all. It forms the vital link between what may seem rather obscure historical scholarship on the one hand, and penetrating studies of current spatial distributions on the other; we need above all, to dissect such all-embracing terms as the 'historical factor', 'historical momentum', 'geographical inertia', and to take a look at the multitude of processes subsumed under such headings. (Harvey, 1967, p. 550.)

2   Introduction to settlement studies in historical geography

At this point the reader may find it useful to refer to Table 1, which summarizes the main concepts dealt with in the whole of this unit. We can look back at the general contrasts between the 'old' and 'new' frameworks of historical geography and some of its continuing characteristics.

Table 1 also enables us to look forward into the remainder of the unit, where the focus is narrowed down to settlement studies, through the work of Wooldridge, Jones, Baker, Porteous and Mills. Wooldridge and Jones were interested in the Anglo-Saxon settlement of England, the one stressing physical factors, the other cultural factors. This contrast is summarized in section 2.1, but the reader may also wish to follow up the references to their original work.

The work of Baker on the distance between farmstead and field and that of Porteous on company towns is contained in full in offprints contained in the correspondence package for this unit. However, the main methodological points arising in these offprints and in Section 3 ('Two kinds of village') are discussed briefly in Section 2.2.

Table 1
Summary of concepts in historical geography mentioned in the text and illustrated in associated extracts and offprints

Concepts	Text	Extracts	(Offprints) Baker	Porteous	Mills (Section 3)
Geographical inertia	1.3	Jones (Section 2)		★	★
Cross sections especially based on sources	1.4.1	Henderson Thomas			★
Vertical themes Evolution	1.4.2	Mitchell			
Historical element Relict features Origins	1.4.3 1.5.3	Prince			★
Importance of physical environment	1.5.1	Wooldridge (Section 2)			
Spatial patterns not also landscape features	1.5	Perry Grigg Jones (Section 2)		★	★★★
Behavioural environment including sociological concepts	1.5.1 2.2	Kirk Jones (Section 2)	★	★★★	★★★
Statistical analysis	1.5.2	Thomas, Perry	★★★	★★	★★
Theory and models	1.5.3	Wrigley	★	★	★★
Theory and change through time	1.5.3	Mitchell Grigg, Harvey		★	
Cross-cultural comparisons	1.5.1	Kirk		★★★	
Distance factors	2.2		★★★		

NOTES

1   In the right hand columns the number of stars has been varied in an attempt to indicate degrees of emphasis on particular concepts.

2   This summary chart is necessarily a simplification of the concepts formerly and currently held by historical geographers. In practice it is often difficult to disentangle, for instance, the search for origins from the concept of geographical inertia.

3   The concepts above the double line were particularly prominent in the 'old' framework of historical geography, but they all continue alongside the concepts below the line, which are associated with the 'new' framework.

4   This summary is *not* to be taken as necessarily representative of the work of the geographers concerned.

2.1   Physical and cultural factors in the Anglo-Saxon settlement of England

Wooldridge was best known as a physical geographer, but he also consciously strove to be a 'whole' geographer and was the joint author, among other items, of a book on the methodology of the subject (1951). The following extract is taken from the first page of his chapter on 'The Anglo-Saxon settlement', which appeared in a book edited by Darby in 1936. It is representative of the spirit in which most geographers at that time addressed themselves to this topic:

> The influence of the physique of Britain on the settlement of the Saxon peoples has been very largely ignored by historians, save in its broader and more evident aspects. . . . From the viewpoint of agricultural settlement it is not only the familiar and relatively static outlines of hill and valley that are important, but also the original vegetation, the soils and the water-supply. For the Saxon settlement was a pioneering venture by an agricultural people, and we must seek to see the country in its former state through the eyes of a practically-minded immigrant farmer. (p. 88.)

Wooldridge then went on to look at the physique of Saxon England for the next eleven pages or so before turning to the nature of the conquest. His approach is to be contrasted with that of G. R. J. Jones (1961) in his 'Basic patterns of settlement distribution in Northern England'.

Although a passing reference is made to the fact that most of the earliest settlements were situated in the lowlands on soils of medium to good quality, Jones is mainly concerned to demonstrate the continuity between the Celtic (Romano-British) and Anglo-Saxon periods. This demonstration requires a frontal assault on the long held assumption that the Celtic way of life was basically pastoral and, therefore, naturally flourished in the moist and less fertile upland areas of Britain, where a dispersed settlement pattern consequently evolved in contradistinction to the nucleated English villages based on communal farming in the drier, more fertile areas. While this assumption was originally made by historians, it was fortified by the simple cause and effect linkage of the early school of environmental determinists.

Jones sustains his argument with a careful assessment of early Welsh records and archaeological evidence, which show that the nucleated hamlet was characteristic of Celtic peoples long before the earliest English colonization. Place name evidence supports the view that the basic English settlement was achieved by taking over existing Celtic villages, where some of the old population was enslaved.

The principal point to notice here is not that physical factors are unimportant. Much that Wooldridge wrote is still very relevant, for Anglo-Saxon farmers, whether they took over old settlements, or migrated short distances from these to start new villages, still required fertile, easily worked soil, a good water-supply and dry sites on which to build their farmsteads. The important point is that a search for direct physical causation led early geographers to neglect significant subtleties, such as those studied by Jones; and in some cases this resulted in their advancing what would now be called 'poor theory'. Neither Jones nor Wooldridge, however, analysed settlement patterns in terms of distance factors. Use of nearest neighbour analysis could produce some interesting results which would bear on the argument that many of the earliest Anglo-Saxon settlements were near Roman and Romano-British settlements. We turn now, therefore, to a brief consideration of distance factors.

2.2   Distance factors and sociological concepts

Students who are familiar with central place theory and more particularly with Chisholm's (1962), *Rural settlement and land use* will be well aware of the importance assigned to distance factors in much recent geographical work. In his offprint Baker (1971) analyses the range of distances separating farm-steads and fields in three nineteenth-century French communes and suggests that a classification of rural settlements 'based on distance factors is more useful than one based on either form or genesis'. He argues that the older classifications of settlement, based mainly on form, tended to be monocausal and, therefore, inadequate. The reader who studies Baker's article may find himself asking whether or not a classification based on distance factors is also monocausal.

It must, of course, be recognized that one of the assets of the 'distance factors' school of thought, is that it strengthens the central core of geographical thinking (Figure 8). In the 1930s, regional geography was the core of the subject; it was here that work done in separate systematic branches was put together in a central body of geographical knowledge. However, in terms of research work, regional geography began a steep decline immediately after the second world war, thus leaving a vacuum at the core of the subject. This has since been occupied by locational analysis, including the 'distance factors' school of thought, which provides a unifying theme by applying similar *techniques* to a wide range of data that geographers need to study (see Unit 1).

Around 1960 it seemed that the systematic branches, which had been ex-panding rapidly, were in danger of separating centrifugally from the core of the subject, but with the coming of the theoretical revolution this danger appears to have passed. In contrast, therefore, to Baker's 'central' paper we offer Porteous' 'peripheral' paper, which introduces the relationship between sociology and settlement geography, within the historical context. Firstly, it is a cross-cultural study, like so much sociological work, in this case the topic being the company towns that originated for several reasons in different countries mainly during the nineteenth century. Secondly, the sociological concept of residential segregation by class, which was common to almost all company towns, is followed through in a detailed case study of Goole.

Figure 8
Illustrating the development of geography over the last few decades.
The increasing size of the cylinders represents the growth in geographical manpower. Note the decrease in the relative size of the central core between 1930 and 1960 and its growth after that date

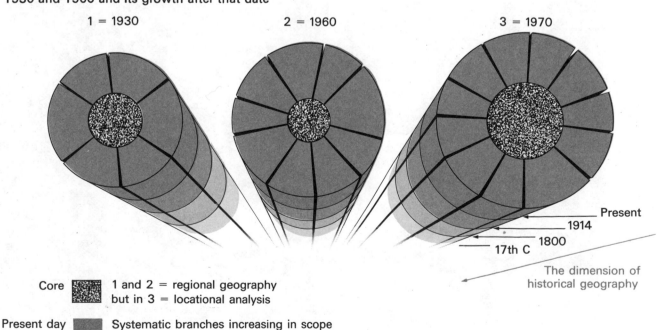

2

4

3

5

6

1. *Woodhouse, Leics: A closed village. The alms-houses erected by Miss Herrick in 1856 for infirm and disabled tradespeople of the parish. Mid-Victorian formality is expressed in the local Charnwood stone and even in such details as doorways (see Figure 2) gates and gardens. From 1594 to 1915 the estate belonged to the Herrick family, the best known of whom was Robert Herrick, the seventeenth century poet*

3. *Woodhouse: A Herrick tomb in the churchyard. More archaeological evidence for the historical geographer*

4. *Woodhouse 'presents a picture of real English rustic beauty, such as is rarely to be met with. All the old houses have been replaced within the last ten years by charming little ornamental cottages . . .' (White's Directory of Leicestershire, 1863 p. 463). The ornaments ran also to exotic evergreens that the peasantry could not afford*

5. *Melbourn, Cambridgeshire: former Methodist chapel and the former Carriers' Arms, the one repre-senting the nonconformity of the open village, the other suggesting a dual occupation of publican and carrier. Photograph by the late William Ogden Copyright, Mrs. M. Ogden, 20 Dolphin La, Melbourn Nr. Royston, Herts*

6. *Hathern. A nonconformist chapel on its cramped site, photographed from inside the churchyard wall. Church and State – chapel and radicalism!*

Readers who press on into Section 3 of this unit will discover certain elements common to the company town and estate villages in rural England. A single controlling influence was an essential characteristic in each case, while different variations on the theme of social segregation occurred in both contexts. The essay in Section 3 makes explicit the role of the sociological concept of social stratification in the study of nineteenth century villages.

By comparison with Baker's article, Porteous and myself have both neglected distance factors. We have preferred to work on the periphery of our subject and have explored the frontier zone between geography, sociology and history. Perhaps it is worth repeating that geography necessarily, like other disciplines, consists of a core area, surrounded by frontier zones, for each is complementary to the other.

Finally, a reference back to Figure 3 reminds us that Kirk's concept of the behavioural environment is also important in these papers, for considerable attention has been paid to 'socio-economic processes and changing environmental values'. The geographical environment has been seen to consist not only of a phenomenal environment of houses, parks, farms, railways, factories and so forth, but also a behavioural environment in which social class, religion, philanthropy and social control were of great importance.

3 Two kinds of village: the use of a model in the historical geography of rural settlement

3.1 Social stratification

3.1.1 Introduction

This topic was discussed in *Understanding Society*, especially by Jeremy Tunstall in Unit 17, *Social Stratification*, where the general concept of national social classes was explored. In Unit 21, John Blunden wrote about *Zoning within cities*, showing us some of the spatial patterns relating to social classes in urban areas.

The present essay is an attempt to follow up some of the same concepts in relation to nineteenth century rural England. It sets out, first, a few points about rural social stratification in general; secondly, an analysis of a selection of social spatial patterns and, thirdly, concludes with a synthesis in the form of a model of rural communities.

3.1.2 Rural social stratification in nineteenth-century England

Table 2 summarizes a very broad description of the rural class structure. Although no attempt has been made to quantify the population in the classes

Table 2   Rural class structure (generalised)

	Class	Description
1	The gentry	= The landed family, members of the squirearchy or the aristocracy
2	Upper middle class	= *a* Professional men, e.g. clergy, doctors, bailiff *b* Gentleman farmers *c* Large tenant farmers
3	Lower or rural middle class	= *a* Yeoman farmers, i.e. small owner-occupiers *b* Tradesmen and craftsmen (masters) *c* Smaller tenant farmers
4	Artisan class	= *a* Estate workers, e.g. carpenter, gamekeeper, butler *b* Journeymen craftsmen working for 3*b* *c* Miscellaneous such as postmen, railway workers, police
5	Labourers	e.g. farm labourers, gardeners, housemaids

listed, in general the numbers grew larger in descending order down the table, while power and status decreased in that direction.

As one would expect, the structure is based very largely on the control of land, but it will be shown below that in certain types of village there were important economic activities that had little connection with rural land use and these had an important modifying effect on the generalized picture presented by Table 2. In effect, these were places where the class structure contained both urban and rural characteristics, thus blurring the so-called traditional distinctions between urban and rural life.

As in Unit 17 of *Understanding Society*, Table 2 is concerned with class (or occupation) status *and* power. The rural clergy are a particularly good example of an occupational group who, partly by virtue of a superior education and partly by virtue of their religious vocation, were able to command a very high status in relation to their parishioners. In the case of the established church this status was underlined by the close links, sometimes of kinship, often of patronage, with the gentry, who also shared with them a common cultural heritage.

Political power was also concentrated in the upper reaches of the class structure. Only in 1884, for example, did the average farm labourer appear on the electoral roll. At the other end of the scale, the gentry and the aristocracy had long had a virtual monopoly of powerful local positions, such as those of magistrate, MP, commissions in the county regiments and local militia and key offices on the boards of guardians, police authorities and the new county and rural district councils.

3.2 Analysis of spatial variations

3.2.1 Ownership of land

The spatial patterns of landownership may be studied at all levels, from that of an individual parish upwards. In his standard work on the landed society, Thompson (1963) has described these patterns at the county level and Figure 9 is based on a small part of his data. This shows, for example, that medium-sized estates were particularly prevalent in the counties surrounding London, as one would expect from the great wealth produced in the City and the consequent demand for country seats at a modest travelling distance from it. Such a pattern is consistent with von Thünen's concept of concentric land use zones round a great city.

On the whole, however, spatial patterns of landownership at the county level are extremely complex and only partially understood. One reason is that counties sometimes contained districts in which quite different conditions prevailed: for example, the growing industrial areas of south Lancashire fell into the same statistical unit as the fells of central and north Lancashire, where land was much cheaper, less fertile and more suitable for the conservation of game.

Any complete explanation of landowning patterns at the level of counties or districts would have to take into account at least the following list of factors:

(a) Type of predominant land use: the grassland farms of the north and west remained small and presented less opportunity for rationalization in large estates than those in the arable areas where farm sizes grew steadily.

(b) In some areas, exceptional soil fertility and/or climatic conditions were linked with arable smallholdings, as in Kent, the Vale of Evesham and the Fens. Here small owner-occupied or rented units were common and together made difficult the growth of large estates in these districts.

(c) In the north of England the defence of the border was possibly a traditional cause of very large estates, especially in Northumberland.

Figure 9
In percentages. *c.* 1870. Distribution of estates of 300–3000 acres

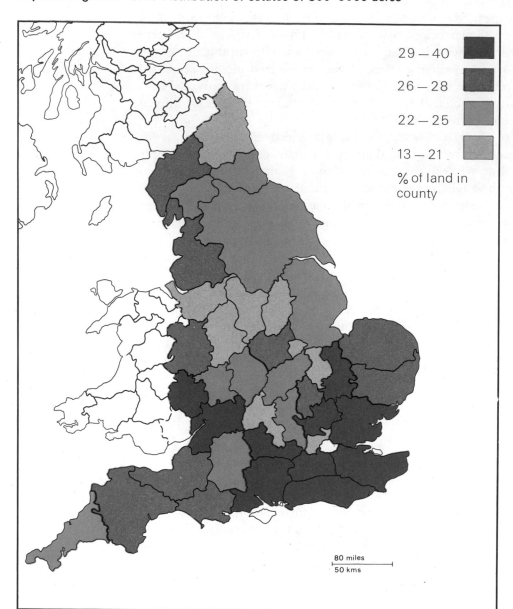

(d)   One might expect to find Welsh influences in the English counties of the border, especially a predilection for small farms and small estates.

(e)   Inheritance customs going back to the colonization period before the Norman Conquest. Where property was shared between several heirs, as in Sussex, Kent and East Anglia, and the tradition persisted into the medieval period, its effects may still have been traceable as late as the nineteenth century.

In the present state of knowledge, however, it is more profitable to concentrate on smaller scale studies, which assist in the construction of a model summarizing the chief characteristics of different types of individual communities.[1] A considerable body of information is available, at this level, from enclosure awards of the eighteenth and nineteenth centuries, tithe awards of the nineteenth century and directories of the period from about 1840.

The land tax assessments are one of the most convenient forms of information, and although they have their deficiencies, they allow us to calculate figures for

---

1   What follows is based very largely on my own research, references to which are cited at the end of the unit.

the density of owners in each township with a reasonable degree of accuracy. Such data are given in Table 3 for a group of 25 townships in south-west Leicestershire, selected for the purpose of exemplifying general ideas and illustrated in Figure 10. The essential point to grasp is that although these villages were situated in a contiguous group and shared common characteristics of soil geography and land use, there were, nevertheless, extremely wide variations in the conditions of landownership from one to the other.

For example, at Elmesthorpe Lady Byron and the Church were the sole owners of land, while the neighbouring townships of Earl Shilton and Barwell were among those where property was divided between over a hundred different proprietors. It is true that Elmesthorpe was a smaller township (in acreage), but the table also makes quite clear that there were wide differences in the *density* of owners. (This figure was arrived at by dividing the township acreage by the number of owners in 1832.) While the table is based on figures for only a small part of one county, there is ample evidence to show that the spatial patterns of landownership were of a like kind in many other parts of England at this period.

Although, as described above, the county gentry of Leicestershire controlled the political apparatus at county level, their degree of both economic and political power varied greatly from one village to another. For example, as magistrates, they set general levels of poor relief, sometimes expressed as so many quartern loaves per person per week, but the day-to-day administration of relief varied greatly from one village to another, as a consequence of purely parochial political and social factors, over which the magistrates had varying degrees of control. The generalized picture of social stratification, as set out in Table 2, was, therefore, also accurate only to varying degrees, depending on parochial circumstances. These are elaborated below as the analysis proceeds.

3.2.2 Farm size and tenure

It is useful to begin, as in 3.2.1, with a quick look at the national picture. In 1851 lowland England had many large farms, while a preponderance of small farms was to be found in the upland counties of the north and west, from Cornwall to Cumberland. This very broad contrast was due to physical conditions and land use as well as to variations in landownership.

In a small area, however, where climate and soil conditions remain relatively constant, the most important variable was landownership, as in the case of our sample of Leicestershire villages (Table 4). Here we see that large estates were associated with large farms, one of the principal reasons being that estate management encouraged entrepreneurial attitudes and these could be more vigorously exploited on larger farm units.

This has important implications for social structure, first because the large tenant farmer had a high economic and social standing in relation to his quite considerable force of labourers; and secondly, because he was dependent on the goodwill of his landlord, both for security of tenure and for improvements on the farm which would enable him to be more productive.

On the other hand, in open townships farms were small, and there were significant numbers of owner-occupiers. The smallness of their family units of production was to some extent offset by their economic and social standing as minor landlords. It will be shown below that lack of opportunity to expand their farming activities sometimes led members of this class into various forms of commercial and industrial enterprise. Their land was important not only for its farming potential, but also as a resource that could be mortgaged, if necessary, to raise capital for non-agricultural activities. Their position within the rural

61

Figure 10
South-West Leicestershire: townships on the Hinckley Ridge

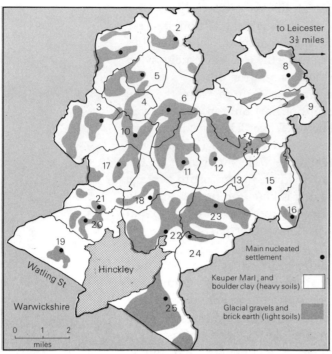

See table 3 for key to village names

Table 3
Villages in south-west Leicestershire: area, owners, population

Key to Figure 10	Name of township	Area		No. of owners c. 1832	Population 1851
		acres	sq. mls		
1	Nailstone	1,954	3·05	8	341
2	Bagworth	2,156	3·36	8	560
3	Market Bosworth	2,716	4·23	8	1,058
4	Osbaston	1,325	2·06	23	227
5	Barlestone	1,067	1·66	44	576
6	Newbold Verdon	1,862	2·91	47	712
7	Desford	2,502	3·90	77	1,025
8	Ratby	3,065	4·80	70	800
9	Kirby Muxloe	1,865	2·90	24	335
10	Cadeby	1,007	1·57	13	179
11	Kirkby Mallory	2,041	3·20	3	261
12	Peckleton	2,180	3·40	38	399
13	Leicester Forest West	309	0·48	No data	50
14	Knoll	232	0·36	4	19
15	Thurlaston	2,575	4·01	40	796
16	Huncote	908	1·41	30	441
17	Sutton Cheney	1,697	2·64	23	340
18	Stapleton	1,365	2·13	31	239
19	Higham-on-the-Hill	2,651	4·15	36	544
20	Stoke Golding	1,291	2·02	45	661
21	Dadlington	1,028	1·59	21	212
22	Barwell	2,387	3·70	113	1,362
23	Earl Shilton	2,077	3·24	106	2,364
24	Elmesthorpe	1,305	2·20	2	45
25	Burbage	3,105	4·85	111	1,951

Townships Numbers 13 and 14, Leicester Forest West and Knoll, have been excluded from further statistical analysis
As extra-parochial areas formed at the enclosure of Leicester Forest they do not share the same settlement history as the other townships. Certain data are also lacking

Numbers of owners: from Land Tax assessments, Leicestershire Record office

Population: 1851 census

Acreages: Index to O.S. Six-Inch Maps, c. 1891. British Museum

Table 4

South-west Leicestershire: Correlation of density of owners with farm size, poor rates, density of population, increases in population, distribution of stocking frames

Township	1 Density of owners 1832		2 Average farm size 1867		3 Poor rate in £ 1847		4 Density of popln 1851		5 Increase in popln 1801–1851		6 Frames per 100 of popln 1844	
	Acs.	Rank	Acs.	Rank	Pence	Rank	PPSM	Rank	%	Rank	No	Rank
Earl Shilton	19	1	38	2	50	1	730	1	83	5	27·0	3
Barwell	21	2	59	7	37½	2	368	3	73	8	29·6	1·5
Barlestone	24	3	34	1	28½	7	348	4	14	21	18·6	7
Burbage	28	4	51	5	28¾	6	403	2	78	6	25·2	4
Stoke Golding	29	5	63	9·5	26¾	8·5	328	5	71	9·5	29·6	1·5
Huncote	30	6	42	3	13½	16	314	6	76	7	21·8	5
Desford	34	7	68	11	30¼	5	262	7	85	4	14·1	9
Newbold Verdon	40	8	49	4	30½	4	245	9	110	2	10·0	11
Ratby	44 } 9·5		88	15·5	21¾	10	168	11	39	12	18·2	8
Stapleton	44 }		70	12·5	16½	14	114	18·5	26	16·5	9·4	12
Dadlington	49	11	70	12·5	10	19	134	13	62	11	18·8	6
Osbaston	58	12	63	9·5	10½	18	110	21	49	12	Nil	20
Peckleton	58	13	106	19	19¾	11	118	16	38	14	Nil	20
Thurlaston	64	14	107	20	15¼	15	198	10	118	1	13·0	10
Higham	74	15	88	5·5	17	13	131	14	26	17·5	0·7	17
Kirby Muxloe	78 } 16·5		60	8	5	22	115	17	101	3	Nil	20
Cadeby	78 }		105	18	35½	3	114	18·5	18	19	4·0	16
Sutton Cheney	82	18	57	6	7½	20	128	15	8	22	4·3	15
Nailstone	244	19	95	17	19½	12	112	20	16	20	Nil	20
Bagworth	270	20	123	21	11¾	17	167	12	71	9·5	6·0	14
Market Bosworth	349	21	79	14	26¾	8·5	250	8	34	15	6·7	13
Elmesthorpe	652	22	208	23	1½	23	20	23	29	16	Nill	20
Kirkby Mallory	682	23	141	22	6	21	81	22	7	23	Nil	20

Correlations of column 1 with column 2 = $+0\cdot750$**
with column 3 = $+0\cdot647$**
with column 4 = $+0\cdot780$**
with column 5 = $+0\cdot472$*
with column 6 = $+0\cdot844$**
** = significant at 99 per cent level
* = significant at 95 per cent level

Sources:

Column 1 Land tax assessments; number of owners divided into acreage (acres per owner)

Column 2 Number of farms recorded in Board of Agriculture Crop Returns, 1867 divided into acreage of township

Column 3 Poor rate in the pound, 1847 from British Parliamentary Paper (House of Commons), 723, 1848

Column 4 Population per square mile based on Census, 1851

Column 5 Census, 1801 and 1851

Column 6 *Report on the condition of the framework knitters*, Royal Commission, 1845, Appendix II, pp. 4–7; and Census, 1841

middle class was further cemented in some cases by marriage alliances with village tradesmen and craftsmen and by worship in the same non-conformist chapels.

3.2.3 Poor rates

The geography of poverty is one of the social spatial patterns the environmental determinist ignored because he could make no direct link between it and the physical geography of an area. However, one relatively longstanding new trend has been the seeking of relationships between spatial patterns of many kinds, without necessarily expecting or looking for a causation in the physical environment.

The Elizabethan poor law was based on the responsibility of individual townships for their poor. Under the strain of industrialization and the marked vicissitudes of trade that it brought, the old poor law gradually broke down. As a consequence, we have inherited a mass of statistical data, much of it in government reports and from this has been selected the 1847 national return of poor rates, which is a most useful indicator of social differences.

Where there were above average levels of expenditure on the poor, one may presume the existence of a large labouring class. Moreover, as most of the rate was borne on agricultural land, rather than on buildings as it is to-day, very high poor rates were often an indication of a large commercial and/or industrial working class not directly dependent on the land. This was true in the Leicestershire villages shown in Table 4, where the current depression in the hosiery trade set up even greater contrasts than one would have found in times of good trade.

Notice, again, that there is a strong correlation with landownership, a correlation that was recognized by Victorian writers on the Poor Law. Here is an example of the importance of the behavioural environment, *as perceived by the persons concerned*. They called the townships of large landowners 'close' or 'closed', because these owners used their control of cottage accommodation to keep down the size of the labouring population. In this way they protected their tenant farmers from high rates, thus making it possible for them to pay a good level of rent. More than this, the tenants of cottages in closed villages were subject to the close social control of squire, parson and farmer. Only respectable workmen, who could be relied upon not to poach or steal food out of the fields, were allowed to remain. For example, at Laxton, in Nottinghamshire, Lord Manvers cleared out a gang of burglars by pulling down the cottages in which they lived.

These families then moved into some of the neighbouring 'open' villages where, in the absence of a single dominating owner, social control was relatively lax. Among the small owners of property in such places were some who ran up rows of third-rate cottages or turned farmhouses into tenements for labouring families. The shortage of accommodation in closed villages was so great in some districts that labourers walked several miles a day between farm and home. Country towns were also involved in these commuting patterns, but, strange to our minds, the direction of movement was outward in the morning and back to the town in the evening.

3.2.4 Population density and growth rates

It may be inferred from what has been said that the population density was higher in open townships than closed (Table 4); it also follows that in a period of general population increase, such as 1750–1850, the differences in population density would get wider. This was true of our Leicestershire sample (Table 4), but as the expansion of the hosiery industry had already spent the greater part

Open and Closed Villages

1. The kennels and stables of the Quorn Hunt, where the fox has ousted the cock. Leicestershire can reasonably claim to have invented fox-hunting, but this was one of several sports indelibly associated with gentry all over the country. Until the late nineteenth century, the taking of game was forbidden even to tenant farmers protecting their own crops. It appears that most poachers lived in the open villages

2. Melbourn: an early nineteenth century cottage in Dolphin Lane. Many of the houses in open villages were poorly constructed and have not survived. Notice the lath and plaster on the gable end and the frail roof timbers

3. Melbourn: a pre-war photograph of the High Street, showing a medley of local building styles and materials.
Photographs by the late Wilfred Ogden. Copyright, Mrs. M. Ogden, 20 Dolphin La, Melbourn, Nr. Royston, Herts.

4. Cusworth Hall, Yorkshire, built 1741–5, photographed 1911. Lady Isabella Battie-Wrightson about to provide afternoon tea for the King's Own Yorkshire Light Infantry. The staff include, from the left, behind the table, a gamekeeper, housemaid, chauffeur, footman, another gamekeeper, head gardener, another housemaid, under-butler, kitchen maid, another under-butler, housemaid, footman, housemaid, gardener, kitchen maid, handyman and a butler. Behind the wing of the table are a housemaid and two gardeners, while in front with Lady Isabella are the lady-in-waiting, the estate steward and the housekeeper and her assistant. This was a community in itself, with a clearly defined hierarchy

The Village was More than the Home of Farmers

West Heslerton, Yorks. The Rev Joseph Henry Hutton getting in the hay in 1892 on glebe land he farmed himself. So the Rector was a dual occupationist and he was assisted by another, Fred Horsley, the village bootmaker, as well as by friends and family. Mr Horsley stands on the top of the rick, wearing a hard hat and the Rector is the bearded patriarchal figure standing to attention. (Copyright of the photograph, Prof. J. H. Hutton; caption based on Gordon Winter's)

Barrow-on-Soar, Leics. The plain, unadorned, but functional dwelling of a village craftsman: the double doors and store shed over suggest that he was perhaps a joiner and undertaker

of its force by 1801, the contrasts did not increase as much as if expansion had continued throughout the nineteenth century.

It is profitable to take the analysis further by looking separately at the three main forms of occupations: agricultural, commercial (or service) and manufacturing. While agricultural employment was more or less uniform per unit area throughout an agricultural district in which the same kind of land use prevailed, it has already been shown that the *residential* patterns of the farm labour force were by no means so uniform.

Therefore the service trades, which depended on the agricultural population for their work, would be attracted to the open villages, where the market was of sufficient size to keep them fully occupied. This attraction was reinforced by the reluctance of large landowners to let many properties in their closed villages to tradesmen, for fear that their workpeople would fall on the rates. Finally, the open villages, with their many small freehold properties were ideally suited to the development of local commerce; indeed, even in late nineteenth century directories one can see many examples of dual occupations, such as farmer and butcher, publican and grazier, and miller and baker, which reflect both the importance of land as a mortgageable asset and the need to have two or more services to offer the restricted hinterland of a central village (see Figure 15).

Such thoughts as these have clear implications for central place theory as outlined in Unit 22 of *Understanding Society*. One of the many factors that guided the development of a pattern of central villages must have been the parallel (historical) development of landowning patterns. This does not, of course, invalidate Christaller's model; it merely complicates it by feeding in another variable, which cannot be quantified in the same way as his other variables. Moreover, it is possible that the interaction of cause and effect went in both directions: open villages may have become central villages, but it is also possible that central villages became open villages in the nineteenth century. For example, many of the large open villages of Leicestershire were situated on

66

or close to the main roads of the county that had been arteries of trade from far back in the medieval period. It is, therefore, a distinct possibility that the peasant land market in these villages developed partly because of the commercial ideas and ideologies caught from passing merchants, as well as because of the more obvious development of a commercial class on important routeways.

Finally, there were many parts of England in which a local craft, such as lace-making, wood-turning, nail-making and the making of boots, developed into a domestic industry of national, or at least regional consequence. We are apt to think of industry as a term synonymous with urban settlement, but many of these industries like the long-established woollen industry, were located substantially in the countryside. The right forms of capital, property and labour were generally found in open villages, where the tradition of local crafts was obviously of prime importance. Of course, we should not neglect the point that where such villages and industries continued to grow through the nineteenth century, usually on the basis of local supplies of coal, the domestic workshop gave way to the mill and the factory and the erstwhile village grew into a town, or if not a town in the full commercial sense, at least into a large industrial village, whose links with agriculture became fainter as time went by.

3.2.5   The distribution of industry

This is such an important topic that the implications of the last paragraph demand amplification. It is, for example, essential to recognize the distinction between extractive and manufacturing industries. Mining and quarrying could only be carried out in areas where the appropriate mineral deposits had been discovered at exploitable depths. The punctiform pattern of mines and quarries gave rise to a similar pattern of new or expanded settlement; these settlements sometimes grew together to make an urban mesh, but in many areas the resource was exhausted before this could happen. The experience of pre-existing open and closed villages would, therefore, vary very greatly according to local circumstances.

However, one common thread can be seen running through the history of most coalfields. Owing to the fact that mineral rights were vested in the landowner in this country (and not in the crown, except for silver and gold) there was a big incentive for the large landowner to interest himself in mining and quarrying and the development of the associated communication network. This was reinforced by the need for large capital sums which rapidly grew beyond the resources of the rural middle class after 1700.

On the other hand, most manufacturing industries, in the domestic phase of the industrial revolution, were labour-intensive, rather than capital- or land-intensive. The large amounts of labour involved made the landed gentry fear increases in both poor rates and poaching and as there was little scope for the use of their capital and land, they were content, for the most part, to leave the development of manufacturing to the middle classes, both rural and urban. An interesting exception occurs in the West Riding woollen industry, where, around 1800, some large proprietors were splitting up relatively large farms into small holdings for weavers. The use of grass fields for bleaching and drying cloth shows, however, that this was a marginal case, as the rents of the original farms, in this poor farming environment, must have been much lower than the combined rents of the weavers' crofts that followed them. (Heaton, 1965, pp. 290–2.)

The class structure of the closed village usually contained nothing to promote industry; the large tenant farmer was expected to employ all his capital on his farm, while the labourer had neither the time nor the money to begin serious side-lines. On the other hand, the small farmer or tradesman or craftsman,

The Hosiery Trade

1

2

1. *Earl Shilton, a village factory in Land Society Lane, an unadopted street, typically unpaved, perhaps originally the responsibility of undercapitalised country builders, certainly a contrast to both the estate village and by-law conscious towns of nineteenth century growth*

2. *Hinckley Road, Earl Shilton: this late nineteenth century terrace is an urban feature in an industrial village. Notice the workpeople going home for the midday meal – the separation of workplace and residence has not gone so far here as in the big towns*

3. *Hinckley Road, Earl Shilton: a piece of archaeological evidence for the historical geographer*

5. *A nineteenth century stocking frame, basically similar to Lee's original machine of c.1600. It was worked by a combination of hand and foot movements,*

3

5

4

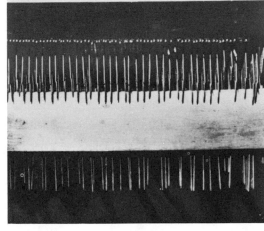

not unlike those needed for the handloom, but as the close-up of the needles shows (see Figure 4) it was a far more sophisticated piece of machinery. Nevertheless, the stockinger was a domestic worker until steam power made small factories necessary about the middle of the nineteenth century. (Photos by courtesy of Atkins Brothers (Hinckley) Ltd.

6. Hathern, Leics. Framework knitting in Leicestershire did not leave behind much archaeological evidence, mainly because most stockingers worked downstairs in the parlour, as shown in the permanent exhibit at the Newarke Museum, Leicester. This house, however, has the looks of a stockinger's cottage because the upstairs windows were obviously enlarged at a later date in a manner comparable to the better known weavers' cottages in Pennine valleys. At any rate, it is a splendid example of vernacular building

6

looking for an outlet for his surplus capital or for the surplus labour of his family was in a good economic position to develop industrial processes. The farmer-cutlers of the Don Valley, the farmer-weavers mentioned above, the farmer-stockingers of the Midlands, various types of farmer-craftsmen in the medieval forests (charcoal burners, ironworkers and arrow makers, for instance) and the present day crofter-weavers of the highlands and islands of Scotland, not to mention the peasant-shipbuilders of Brittany, are all examples of dual occupations that have played an important part in industrialization, probably beyond their actual weight of numbers.

Focusing attention briefly on Leicestershire; when the stocking frame was introduced in the seventeenth century, it was too expensive for the labourer to buy, but was within the reach of farmers and tradesmen. During the eighteenth century there was a rapid growth of the industry which led to the proletarianization of the labour force; but the location, as far as we can be sure, was still in 1844 in those open villages where it had first begun its expansion from the organizing market centres of Hinckley, Leicester and Loughborough-Shepshed. In the extreme right hand column of Table 4 the distribution of stocking frames shows a correlation, as we would now expect, with the density of owners.

At this date, the hosiery trade was on the eve of factory organization and although this led to some concentration on the towns, the principle of geographical inertia, reinforced by the coming of newer industries such as footwear and light engineering, has kept the pattern of industrial villages much the same down to the present day. The main new factor has been the spread of suburbanization to villages within sufficiently close proximity of the main towns: thus Earl Shilton, Barwell, Burbage and Stoke Golding, although still discrete settlements, have long since been absorbed into the Hinckley Urban District.

3.3 A model

3.3.1 The open-closed dichotomy

Having analysed some of the most significant spatial variables, an attempt is now made to synthesize the material round the dichotomy that existed between open and closed villages. The closed villages were those controlled by one or

Figure 11
Sociological classification of villages

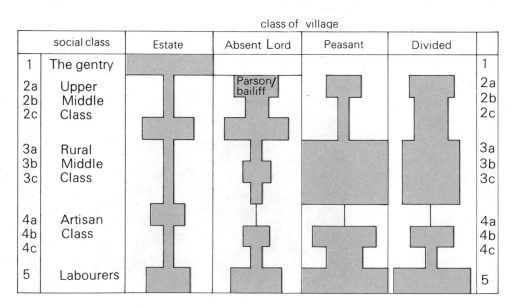

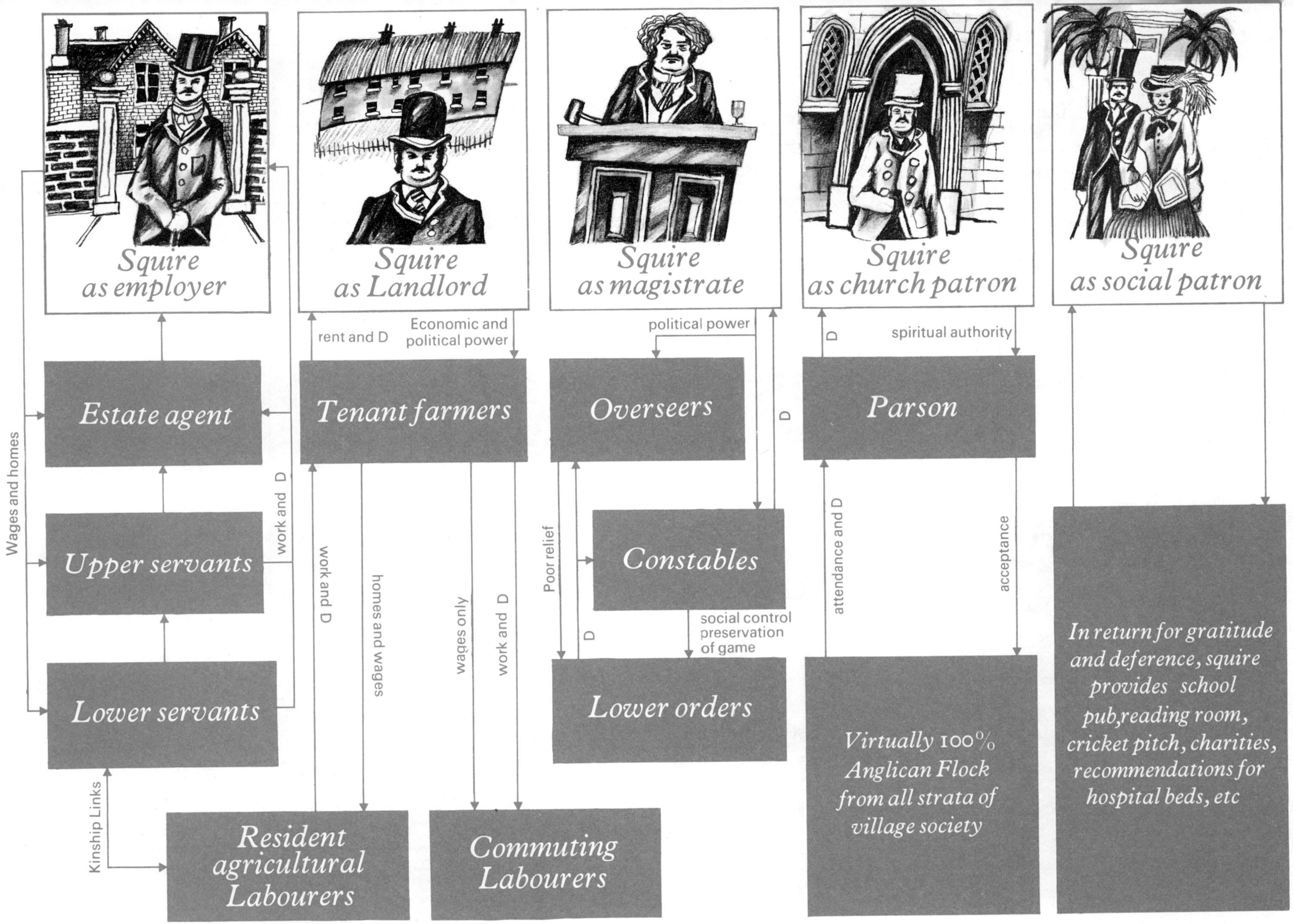

Figure 12
The Estate village as a closed system

D Deference to higher strata

Figure 13
An open network: tenural, social and economic relationships in a peasant village

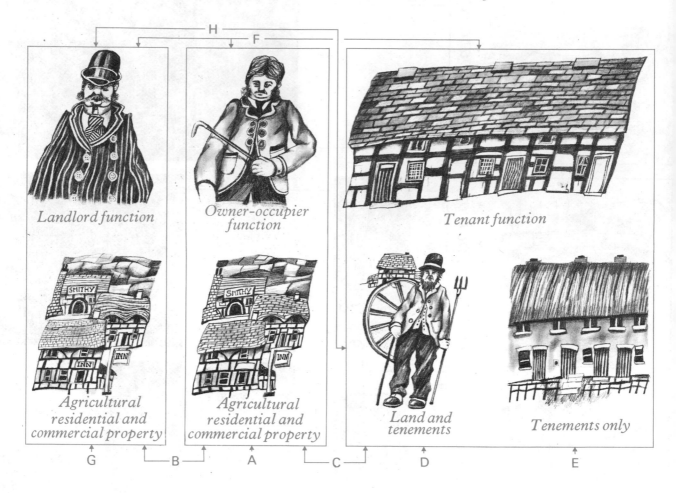

Landlord function

Owner-occupier function

Tenant function

Agricultural residential and commercial property

Agricultural residential and commercial property

Land and tenements

Tenements only

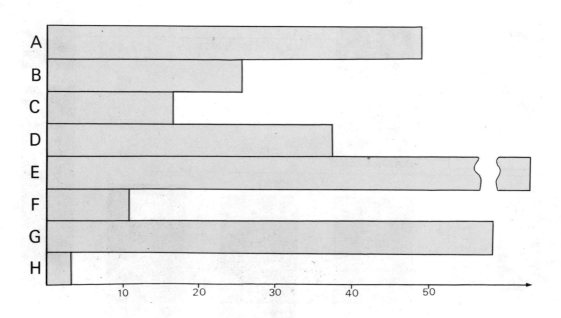

two large landowners, who, characteristically owned over two-thirds, often over 95 per cent of the property. In Figure 11 it can be seen that they have been divided again between those where the owner was resident (estate villages) and those where he was not (absentee landlord townships). The mere fact of residence was extremely important because it brought all strata of society into contact with the landed family. Here was the centre of a large block of property, often extending through several parishes, where a mansion had been built in a park surrounded by pleasure and kitchen gardens, stables, icehouses and lodges, mausoleums and the family church. The visual impact of the estate village, especially, perhaps, its model cottages and single public house emblazoned with the arms of the manorial lord, even in its decayed form of the 1970s, is unmistakeable to the most casual observer. The impact of the absent landowner on his more distant properties was equally real, but less forceful and much more easily erased by the passage of time.

As the Leicestershire data show, there could be a very wide variation in the number of separate owners and even when the closed villages are removed from the range, it still often ran from a dozen or so up to well over 100 owners. In Figure 11, therefore, a more or less arbitrary distinction is represented between the peasant village, with many owners, including significant numbers of owner-occupiers, on the one hand, and the village that was more simply 'divided', on the other. The divided village did not have such a well developed rural middle class, it may have contained the seat of a minor landed family, such as that of a retired service officer, and it was unlikely to sport such a wide variety of shops and workshops, nonconformist chapels and community organisations as the larger peasant village.

If the four parts of Figure 11 were to be combined, there would result a diagrammatic representation of social stratification in rural England as a whole. As we have seen, however, each stratum had its own spatial patterns and these are represented with tolerable accuracy in the four separate sections of Figure 11 as it stands.

3.3.2 A closed system and an open network

Figures 12 and 14 show in greater detail how the estate village worked as a closed economic, political and social system, in which all parts were interdependent on the others, but the overriding fact was the dependence of all the lower social strata on the resident family. As in an enlightened despotism, every single aspect of life, economic, political, judicial, social, religious and educational came under the scrutiny of the squire, either directly through his own participant observation or that of his most trusted servants. Here was the rural equivalent of the select upper middle class quarters of the growing industrial cities of the same period.

On the other hand, the peasant village (Figures 13 and 15) was characterized by a much looser network. It was open to entry at many points of the inter-locking network of economic, tenurial and social relationships. A man might have two occupations, he could be both tenant and landlord, he was not confined to the Established church on Sundays, he could and did dare to be radical in his politics, but he often paid for these 'rights' and 'privileges' by working harder than the estate servant and living in less attractive and less healthy housing. Nevertheless, he could move about the network, playing different roles, sometimes being subordinate, sometimes leader, while in the closed villages everyone knew his 'place'.

So far, this model has concentrated on the classification of villages. Although a classification, especially if generalized, may be regarded as a model, it clearly becomes more effective as a model if it also deals with cause and effect links and if it can be used for predictive purposes. Space precludes a full

Figure 14
Causal links in the closed village

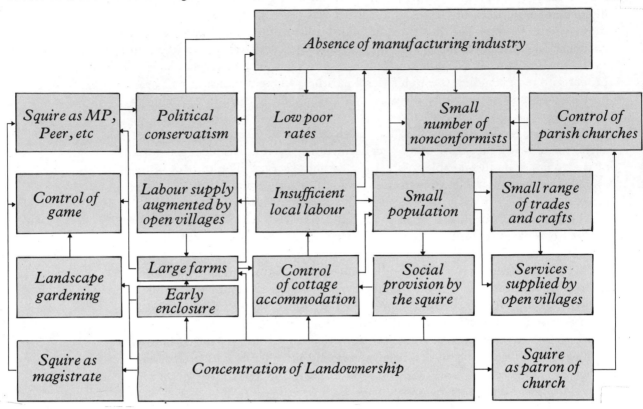

discussion of these aspects of the subject, but enough may be said to show that this model is potentially normative as well as descriptive – 'it deals with what might be expected to occur under certain stated conditions' (Chorley and Haggett, 1967, p. 25.)

Figures 14 and 15 are intended to summarize the causal links associated with this model. For example, in Figure 14, a chain of links leads from the concentration of ownership to the early enclosure of common fields, which facilitated the arrangements of tenancies in large farms, the layout of woods, park, fox coverts and so forth and, hence, one found good conditions for the preservation of game. Likewise, in Figure 15, the dispersal of control over land

Figure 15
Causal links in the open village

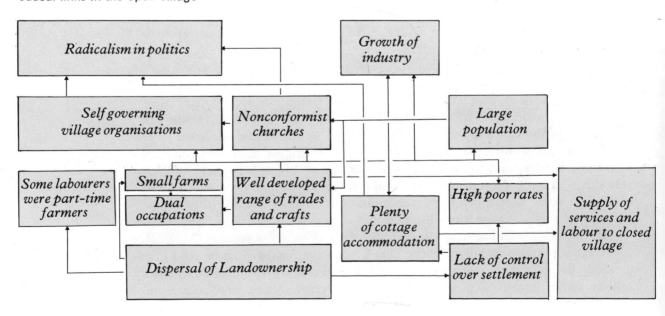

was the principal cause of lack of control over Settlement (in the poor law sense) and this, in turn, was related to the free availability of accommodation, high poor rates and, making a bigger assumption, to radicalism in politics. These two diagrams are extremely generalized. One knows, for example, that early enclosure, say before 1700, was not confined to closed townships. A more thorough discussion would bring out many other qualifications, but the suggestions made in the diagrams are by no means untenable.

To what degree is the model predictive, i.e. given the period of application as the nineteenth century, will the open-closed dichotomy have the same force in other parts of Britain, especially in England? Provided we recognize the fact that industry was more highly developed in Leicestershire than in some parts of the country, the model has a considerable relevance in many localities. Readers may refer to the published work of several historians and geographers, which indicates that the model has varying degrees of fit, generally quite close, in widely separated parts of the country.[1]

3.3.3 How does such a model enhance geographical understanding?

A model that draws in so much from the fields of other social sciences needs to be justified in the context of geographical study. Quite simply, the justification is that we cannot hope to have a full understanding of spatial patterns within and between villages, unless we take into account all the different factors having an impact on them, and not merely those of the phenomenal environment.

However, the final judgement of a teaching model is based on the balance between the student's increased understanding of basic issues on the one hand and any loss of willingness on his part to go on observing the real world for himself on the other hand. Perhaps you would like to ponder this.

1 For Warwickshire see Ashby (1961) and Arch (1967); for Berkshire, Havinden (1966); for Cheshire, Sylvester (1949); for Norfolk, Springall (1936); for Bradford, Mortimore (1969); for Leeds, Ward in Baker et al. (1970); for Lincolnshire, Rogers (1969); and for Nottinghamshire, Mills (1970). On Oxfordshire and Bedfordshire, I base my remarks on letters from Mr. John Walton and Mr. Peter Grey respectively, who are researching on these counties. The Scots could turn to Third (1955), Lebon (1946), Houston (1948), or Geddes (1951); while Welsh students may find it interesting to look at an urban application (Llandudno) in Carter and Davis (1970) pp. 66–78, or at another model of mining communities, in P. N. Jones (1969).

References

ARCH, J. (1967) *The autobiography of Joseph Arch*, abridged edition, London, MacGibbon and Kee.

ASHBY, M. K. (1961) *Joseph Ashby of Tysoe*, London, Routledge & Kegan Paul.

BIRRELL, J. (1969) 'Peasant craftsmen in the medieval forest', *Agricultural History Review*, 17, pp. 91–107.

BAKER, A. R. H., HAMSHERE, J. D. and LANGTON, J. (eds.) (1970) *Geographical Interpretations of Historical Sources: Readings in Historical Geography*, Newton Abbot, David and Charles.

BAKER, A. R. H. (ed.) (1972) *Progress in historical geography*, Newton Abbot, David and Charles.

BALCHIN, W. G. V. (1954) *The making of the English landscape: Cornwall*, London, Hodder and Stoughton.

BROEK, J. O. M. (1932) *The Santa Clara Valley, California*, Utrecht, Oosthoek Uitgevers—Miji., A.

CARTER, H. and DAVIS W. K. D. (eds.) (1970) *Urban essays: studies in the geography of Wales*, London, Longman.

CHISHOLM, M. (1962) *Rural settlements and land use*, London, Hutchinson.

CHORLEY, R. J. and HAGGETT, P. (eds.) (1967) *Models in geography*, London, Methuen.

CONSTANT, A. (1948) 'The geographical background of inter-village population movements in Northamptonshire and Huntingdonshire, 1754–1943', *Geography*, 33, 78–88.

DARBY, H. C. (ed.) (1936) *An Historical geography of England before 1800*, Cambridge, Cambridge University Press.

DARBY, H. C. *et al.*, (eds.) *The Domesday geography of England*, six volumes, Cambridge, Cambridge University Press.

GEDDES, A. (1951) 'Changes in rural life and landscape: 1500–1950' in Robertson, C. J. (ed.) *Scientific survey of south east Scotland*, Edinburgh, British Association for the Advancement of Science.

GREGORY, S. (1968) *Statistical methods and the geographer*, second ed., London, Longman.

GRIGG, D. B. (1962) 'Changing regional values during the agricultural revolution in south Lincolnshire', *Transactions of the Institute of British Geographers*, 30, pp. 91–103.

HARRIS, A. (1970) *The rural landscape of the East Riding of Yorkshire 1700–1850*, London, Reprinted S.R. Publications, Wakefield.

HARTSHORNE, R. (1959) *Perspective on the nature of geography*, Chicago, Rand McNally.

HARVEY, D. (1967) 'Models of the evolution of spatial patterns in human geography' in Chorley, R. J. and Haggett, P. (eds.) (1967) *Models in Geography*, London, Methuen.

HAVINDEN, M. A. (1966) *Estate Villages*, London, Lund Humphries.

HEATON, H. (1965) *The Yorkshire woollen and worsted industries*, London, Oxford University Press (second edition).

HENDERSON, H. C. K. (1952) 'Agriculture in England and Wales in 1801', *Geographical Journal*, 118, pp. 338–45.

HEY, D. D. (1969) 'A dual economy in South Yorkshire', *Agricultural History Review*, 17, pp. 108–19.

HOUSTON, J. M. (1948) 'Village planning in Scotland 1745–1845', *Advancement of Science*, 5, pp. 129–32.

JONES, G. R. J. (1961) 'Basic patterns of settlement distribution in Northern England', *Advancement of Science*, 17, pp. 192–200.

JONES, P. N. (1969) *Colliery settlement in South Wales coalfield, 1850–1926*, Hull, University of Hull Occasional Papers in Geography, No. 14.

KIRK, W. (1951) 'Historical geography and the concept of the behavioural environment', *Indian Geographical Journal*, Silver Jubilee volume, pp. 152–60.

KIRK, W. (1963) 'Problems of geography', *Geography*, 48, pp. 357–71.

LEBON, J. H. G. (1946) 'The process of enclosure in the western lowlands', *Scottish Geographical Magazine*, 62, pp. 100–10.

MILLS, D. R. (1959) 'The development of rural settlement around Lincoln', *East Midland Geographer*, 11, pp. 3–15.

MILLS, D. R. (1959) 'Enclosure in Kesteven', *Agricultural History Review*, 7, pp. 82–97.

MILLS, D. R. (1959) 'The poor laws and the distribution of population', *Transactions of the Institute of British Geographers*, 26, pp. 185–95.

MILLS, D. R. (1963) *Landownership and rural population with special reference to Leicestershire in the mid-nineteenth century*, University of Leicester unpublished Ph.d. thesis.

MILLS, D. R. (1965–6) 'English villages in the eighteenth and nineteenth centuries: a sociological approach', *Amateur* (now *Local*) *Historian*, 6, pp. 271–8 and 7, pp. 7–13.

MILLS, D. R. (1970) 'The geographical effects of the laws of settlement in Nottinghamshire', *East Midland Geographer*, 5, pp. 31–8.

MILLWARD, R. (1955) *The making of the English landscape: Lancashire*, London, Hodder and Stoughton.

MITCHELL, J. B. (1954) *Historical geography*, London, English Universities Press.

MORTIMORE, M. J. (1969) 'Landownership and urban growth in Bradford 1850–1950', *Transactions of the Institute of British Geographers*, 46, pp. 105–19.

OPEN UNIVERSITY SOCIAL SCIENCES FOUNDATION COURSE TEAM (eds.) (1970) *Understanding society: readings in the social sciences*, London, Macmillan.

OPEN UNIVERSITY SOCIAL SCIENCES FOUNDATION COURSE TEAM (eds.) (1971) *Money, Wealth and Class*, D100 Units 14–18, Bletchley, Open University Press.

OPEN UNIVERSITY SOCIAL SCIENCES FOUNDATION COURSE TEAM (eds.) (1971) *Spatial Aspects of Society*, D100 Units 19–22, Bletchley, Open University Press.

PAHL, R. E. (1967) 'Sociological models in geography' in Chorley, R. J. and Haggett, P., *Socio-economic models in geography*, London, Methuen.

PAHL, R. E. (1970) *Patterns of urban life*, London, Longman.

PEEL, R. F. (1942) 'Local intermarriage and the stability of the rural population in the English Midlands', *Geography*, 27, 21–30.

PERRY, P. J. (1969) 'Working class isolation and mobility in rural Dorset, 1837–1936: a study of marriage distances', *Transactions of the Institute of British Geographers*, 46, pp. 121–41.

PORTEOUS, J. D. (1970) 'The nature of the company town', *Transactions of the Institute of British Geographers*, 51, pp. 127–42.

PRED, A. R. (1966) *The spatial dynamics of U.S. urban-industrial growth, 1800–1914: interpretive and theoretical essays*, Cambridge, Massachusetts, M.I.T. Press.

PRINCE, H. C. (1964) 'The origin of pits and depressions in Norfolk', *Geography*, 49, pp. 15–32.

ROGERS, A. (ed.) (1969) *Stability and change: Some aspects of North and South Rauceby, Lincolnshire, in the nineteenth century*, Nottingham, University of Nottingham, Department of Adult Education.

SPRINGALL, L. M. (1936) *Labouring life in Norfolk villages, 1834–1914*, London, Allen and Unwin.

SYLVESTER, D. (1949) 'Rural settlement in Cheshire', *Transactions of the Historical Society of Lancashire and Cheshire*, 101, pp. 1–37.

THIRD, B. M. W. (1955) 'Changing landscapes and social structure in the Scottish Lowlands', *Scottish Geographical Magazine*, 71, pp. 83–93.

THOMAS, D. (1959) 'The acreage returns of 1801 for the Welsh Borderland', *Transactions of the Institute of British Geographers*, 26, pp. 169–83.

THOMAS, D. (1967) 'Climate and cropping in the early nineteenth century in Wales' in Taylor, J. A. (ed.), *Weather and agriculture*, Oxford, Oxford University Press.

THOMPSON, F. M. L. (1963) *English landed society in the nineteenth century*, London, Routledge and Kegan Paul.

VINCE, A. (1966) *Entre Loire et Vilaine: la population dans la presqu'ile guerandaise*, Université de Poitiers, Thèse de géographie humaine.

WOOLDRIDGE, S. W. and EAST, W. G. (1951) *The Spirit and purpose of geography*, London, Hutchinson.

WRIGLEY, E. A. (ed.) (1966) *An introduction to English historical demography*, London, Weidenfeld and Nicolson.

WRIGLEY, E. A. (1967) 'A simple model of London's importance in changing English society and economy, 1650–1750', *Past and Present*, 37, pp. 44–70.

Acknowledgements

Grateful acknowledgement is made to the following sources for material used in this unit:

TEXT

Cambridge University Press for S. W. Wooldridge, 'The Anglo-Saxon Settlement' in H. C. Darby (ed.) *An Historical Geography of England Before 1800*; English Universities Press for J. B. Mitchell, *Historical Geography*; The Geographical Association for W. Kirk, 'Problems of geography' in *Geography*, 48 and for H. C. Prince, 'The origin of pits and depressions in Norfolk' in *Geography*, 49; Institute of British Geographers for D. B. Grigg, 'Changing regional values during the agricultural revolution in south Lincolnshire' in *Transactions*, 30; Methuen for D. Harvey, 'Models of the evolutions of spatial patterns in human geography' in R. J. Chorley and P. Haggett (eds.) *Models in Geography*; The Past and Present Society, Corpus Christi College, Oxford for E. A. Wrigley, 'A simple model of London's importance in changing English society and economy, 1650–1750' in *Past and Present*, 37; Rand McNally for R. Hartshorne, *Perspective on the Nature of Geography*.

FIGURES

The Geographical Association for Fig. 2 from H. C. Prince, 'The origins of pits and depressions' in *Geography*, 49, 1963 and for Fig. 3 in W. Kirk, 'Problems of geography' in *Geography*, 48, 1963; The Institute of British Geographers for Figs. 5 and 6, from D. Thomas, 'The average returns of 1801 for the Welsh borderland' in *Transactions*, 26, 1959; The Past and Present Society, Corpus Christi College, Oxford for Fig. 7 from E. A. Wrigley, 'A simple model of London's importance 1650–1970'. The figure is reprinted with the permission of the Society and the author from *Past and Present, a journal of historical studies*, 37. World Copyright.

Routledge & Kegan Paul for Fig. 9 from F. M. C. Thompson, *English landed Society in the Nineteenth Century*; The Royal Geographical Society for Fig. 4, from H. C. K. Henderson, 'Cereal crops in Herefordshire, 1801' in *Geographical Journal*, 1952.

Regional geography to regional analysis

Unit 15   Andrew Learmonth (part one) Vida Godson (part two)

Unit 15   Contents

Part one   Introduction and perspective

1   Aims

(i)   To gather together various references to regional geography already made in the course, rather than to launch the student on a lot of reading of traditional regional geography (though indicating some entry points into the literature for students who want to do that).

(ii)   To show how attempts to apply regional geography, or even to apply traditional systematic geography to regional problems, lead very strongly towards the interdisciplinary area often called regional science.

(iii)   To illustrate the nature of the regional science approach by selected examples, and to give some entry points into the literature.

2   Students' objectives

(i)   The student should refresh his memory about the merits and limitations of at least one piece of traditional regional geography (but should not begin any substantial reading programme in the field). Guidance is given in paragraph 4.2 below.

(ii)   He should be able to cite examples of the *type* of information and the type of conclusion or recommendation obtained when one tries to use traditional regional geography in solving regional problems. The television broadcast and the offprint by Learmonth should help students; the use of other sources or experience is by no means excluded but do found any discussion upon evidence not polemics.

(iii)   He should follow the arguments in the specially written paper by Vida Godson which comprises the main part of the unit: if necessary select one of the tools she describes for particular study. However, there is no need to memorize formulas etc. For examination purposes, as in real life problems, if a formula is necessary to solve a problem it can be looked up (or provided in an examination paper); this is much better than depending on memory. It is important to be able to use a few simple formulas, mentioned in the unit. Appropriate aids to numerical calculations, again, will be given.

3   Traditional regional geography

3.1   Our emphasis in this course

We think that many students will already have much knowledge and experience of traditional regional geography, from school days, from teaching experience or from general reading. Moreover we have already discussed this type of geography to some extent earlier in the course, and to a lesser extent in the Foundation Course D100 *Understanding Society*. And we are very conscious that the later discussion of regional analysis may occupy a very large proportion of the time the student can allot to this unit. So this introductory section will be almost exclusively concerned with pulling together earlier references to traditional regional geography in the somewhat different context of this unit.

3.2   Entry points into the literature

As in many parts of this course, we thought that entry points into the literature might help many students who do not have much previous acquaintance with it. *But in order to stress that you are NOT expected to explore the literature widely as part of this course, we include our note on this with the References.*

4   A retrospect upon earlier references to regional geography in this course

4.1   Foundation Course D100 Unit 4, *Understanding Society*

Our treatment was so brief that we don't suggest that students who did *not* do the course should go out of their way to get this unit. But if you have your copy, it might be worthwhile to re-read the paragraphs of the Appendix 'Geography in the 1970s: one man's retrospect and prospect'. In a sentence, we suggested that for a time many geographers claimed regional geography as *the* culminating synthesis of geographical studies, as a holistic study (greater than the sum of its parts) to which all other branches of geography were tributary. But we added that regional geography had been in some disrepute for a good many years now, because of overstated claims for it, and for various other reasons.

4.2   Block I of the present course—'Evolution or Revolution in Geography?'

On pp. 11–15 of the correspondence text we invited you to look at the chapter on the London Basin by G. H. Dury (1968), and pp. 12–13, as well as the earlier part of the television programme, were intended to help. On p. 14 we invited you to assess the different parts of Dury's chapter from the point of view of description, analysis, interrelationships and synthesis. If you have not been able to get access to Dury's book you may care to spend a limited time, say up to an hour, applying p. 14 to any other regional essay you do have available. From this we hope you will have some sense of vicarious participation in regional geography.

On pp. 16–17, and in the reprinted extracts from *Strategic Plan for the South East*, we invited your attention to a study culminating in an official report. This includes much in common with traditional regional geography, but also more that is based on complex calculations, often using computers, as a basis for forecasting, than is as yet common in writings on regional geography.

With these readings in your mind, we then invited you to look more analytically at the geographer's handling of data in Unit 2 of the block, 'Geographic data and methods'. You will find some relevant points in 2.3, 'Modes of studying patterns' and in 2.4, 'The study of functional relationships'. There is an important specific discussion in 3, 'Regional geography' (pp. 44–6). The important trend is the widespread dissatisfaction with what one might call arts-type, literary and largely descriptive syntheses using judgement or subjective integration and with the study of the unique in geography, rather than the law-responsive. (Widespread is not universal – see Minshull (1967), already cited above, or Fisher (1970).) On the other hand section 4.1.4, 'Regionalization', in a very real sense accomplished some of the work of this present unit on the theme of 'regional geography to regional analysis'. Here we find an expression of the preference for the search for the law-responsive rather than the regionally unique. In places the more broadly philosophic approach of Unit 3 'why has geography changed', is also relevant (see pp. 60–2).

In rather a different way, we may build on Learmonth's radio broadcast on *One geographer's progress 1945–71*, and on the television programme for this unit and with the same title, *Regional geography to regional analysis*. For those unable to see the television programme, or as an ancillary to it, the offprint of Learmonth (1964) in the supplementary materials for this section of the course may prove helpful. The second part of the television broadcast is based on pp. 415–9 of Isard (1960) on a graphical solution using linear programming to a simplified and hypothetical problem in choice of combinations of two industries using different quantities of water, land, labour and capital in a region with restricted resources of these four requirements and with the objective of maximizing new income based on manufacturing. Isard's presentation is reproduced, with permission, as an offprint included with the supplementary material. The television programme is based simply on a step by step and animated presentation of the same graphs.

5 Towards regional analysis

With Isard's graphical presentation of a linear programming solution to a problem of alternative choices in regional development we have moved from regional geography to regional analysis, and are ready to go on to the main content of this unit, a brief exposition of selected techniques of regional analysis by Mrs. Vida Godson, a former student of Isard.

We have included a number of footnotes on several pages of Vida Godson's essay. These are intended as guidance to students new to the field, and for such students we would rank these as essential reading.

Part two   Aspects of regional analysis

1   Introduction

1.1   The need for regional analysis

At the beginning of this course we discussed changes in geographic thought which have resulted in a diminished concern on the part of geographers for the production of synthetic regional descriptions as an end in themselves (see Block 1, Unit 2). But, although we can no longer support the idea of a natural partitioning of the earth's surface into regions which may be 'recognized' by the trained eye and which have an existence over and above any specific study purpose, we concluded that the concept of a region which is either homogeneous or focused with respect to a particular set of variables under study must persist as a method of defining meaningful spatial units of analysis. The important consideration is not which boundaries are chosen but the effects of this choice on the variables under study. However, a spatial unit of analysis is in effect a primitive or original concept for geography and thus justifies our continuing use of regions as study elements in many cases. Moreover a demand for analysis of regional units has been thrust upon geographers from outside the discipline. The pressing demands of regional planning councils and other bodies concerned with regional welfare disparities have resulted in the gradual accumulation of an assortment of theories and techniques which are now often known collectively as regional analysis.

Regional specialization and hence disparities are inherent in even quite primitive economies (see the first section of Block 2 of this course) and the accentuation of these disparities is a natural accompaniment of economic development. Thus the 'regional problem' is a feature which has been marked since the industrial revolution, but nevertheless the idea of government intervention to control such inequalities is very much more recent and in the British case has its origins only in the 1930s. This may seem astonishing but it must be remembered that the goals of full employment and the welfare state which are a common spur to a government's acceptance of the need for regional policies are themselves little older than this.

Much of the following argument assumes acceptance of the need in many contexts for regional planning. Not all, of course, would accept this assumption. It has been suggested that there is some evidence that regional disparities are at their greatest at an intermediate stage of development. However, in most developed economies today it is possible to recognize three major types of regional problem: first, the backward agricultural region commonly suffering from over-population, an archaic land holding system, low capitalization, primitive agricultural methods and consequently an unsophisticated work force; second, the area of declining heavy industry which is burdened with an outmoded urban and industrial infra-structure and a large semi-skilled work force which is difficult to retrain; third, the congested region like the south-east of England or the Washington-New York corridor of the United States, where rapid growth has resulted in extreme social and economic pressures and where further development entails very high social costs and disproportionate public investment. Each of these types of region requires specific local treatment but the problems of the three types are inter-dependent and many of the keys to their solution must lie in policies of action which operate directly on these interdependencies.

Assuming then a political climate favouring planning, the regional policy maker requires information which exceeds that provided by traditional regional geography in four respects:

(i) He requires better tools for regional description. The old style verbal portrait is no longer sufficient. The policy maker needs quantitative statements which will allow him to *evaluate* regional characteristics, especially socio-economic ones, and compare them both over time and with other regions. He needs measures of the degree of industrial concentration, the extent of employment shifts from one sector to another, and so on.

(ii) The planner needs much more than the synthetic description based on subjective judgement which was the ambition of the regional geographer. He requires *theories* which attempt to explain the working of regional scale space economies and from which he can identify points of leverage through which to implement his policies.

(iii) The interdependencies between the problems of different regions require analysis at a broader level than hitherto. In addition to the customary intra-regional analyses we need explicit treatment of inter-regional aspects such as inter-regional migrations and trade flows.

(iv) The applied nature of current demands means that we need to go not merely beyond regional descriptions to regional theories but even beyond this to provide 'prescriptive' models which will assist the planner to prescribe remedies and to make rational decisions. The planner needs models which will help him to decide how much investment to direct towards different sectors of the economy, how many miles of motorway to construct, or what level of tax incentive to provide to bring about a desired result.

1.2 Recent changes in regional studies

Regional analysis was slow to get off the ground not only because of the lack of demand from policy makers but also because there were various academic constraints on its development. As we have said, regional geography was held back for a long time by its commitment to synthetic description and this effectively precluded the development of both theory and inter-regional work. At the same time, however, much economics theory was also constrained by a disciplinary commitment to theories based on the assumption of perfect competition. The straitjacket of this assumption held up the progress of work in regional economics because by assuming perfect competition, and thus concentrating on models which describe equilibrium states of the economy, one assumes away the problem of regional disparities as nothing more than temporary time lags in the adjustment of the system.

Economics has of course been shaking itself free of this philosophy for some while now and recognition of the facts of imperfect availability of information about economic conditions and the risky environment in which all economic decisions must be made now allows scope for acknowledging that, for example, investment opportunities in a lagging region may not be recognized by entrepreneurs and thus 'natural' adjustments may not operate to counteract emerging regional disparities in the way which was previously thought to be inevitable. Thus regional economics is now a rapidly expanding field but nevertheless the climate within economics departments was sufficiently bad as late as the 1950s for Walter Isard to feel it necessary to found a new discipline outside economics to study regional problems. Throughout the 1950s and early '60s the majority of work on regional analysis stemmed from Isard's Regional Science department and it is only very recently that researchers in economics and geography departments have taken up the lead from this source.

The adoption of regional analysis into geography has been particularly slow and it is in fact only within the last few years that it has come to be commonly accepted. Its acceptance as a legitimate concern of geographers has been brought about gradually as the result of increasing systematic study by economic geographers to the point where recognition of the continuity of the theories of regional economists and economic geographers has become inevitable. It would, however, be misleading to suggest that regional analysis is merely the blending of regional economics and economic geography for it is potentially much more than this and Professor Isard is again leading the two disciplines on, pointing the way towards study not just of the regional economic system but of the combined social, political and economic spatial system. (See Isard, W., *et al.*, 1969.)

1.3 The scope of regional analysis

As we have already indicated in Section 1.1, the demands of regional policy makers require that the regional analyst should work at both intra-regional and inter-regional levels to produce better quantitative descriptions, theories and prescriptive models. In Block 2 of this course we have already discussed many intra-regional issues and particularly micro level models describing the location behaviour of individual industrial plants, since these topics have always lain squarely within the province of systematic studies in economic geography. An argument could easily be made out that such topics should now be entirely subsumed under the new title of regional analysis, but it would not be worthwhile to pursue such a dialogue, for the jurisdiction of the various administrative sub-branches of geography, or for that matter social science, is of no lasting concern. You should, however, recognize that much material germane to regional analysis has already been discussed in Block 2 (and in Units 19 to 22 of the Foundation Course *Understanding Society*) and you should bear that work in mind whilst studying this unit. As location theory has already been covered we will concentrate here on those aspects of regional analysis which have not previously been considered by geographers, that is, on the macro models of the working of the system at regional and inter-regional levels and on the scope for prescriptive models in this context. However, even restricting ourselves just to these areas we cannot hope to give a comprehensive introductory coverage to all the major topics handled by regional analysts and will, therefore, have to restrict ourselves to discussing just two or three of them which will, we hope, give an indication of the sorts of material treated and the types of technique currently in use.

2 Economic base models and multiplier analysis

2.1 Economic multipliers and impact analysis [1]

Like national economies, regional and even local economies tend over time to experience quite violent ups and downs in their prosperity, and although some of these oscillations are undoubtedly the result of fluctuations inescapable in a relatively unplanned economy, it is thought that some at least may be avoidable or correctable. Thus economists have long been interested in studying factors which appear to generate these cycles. In particular they have been attracted by the question of the influence of changes in investment on changes in total income and employment because the volume of investment is one of

1 Editor's Note: Many of you know from experience that a piece of economic development, say the opening of a factory making calculating machines in a depressed area, has an impact on the economy of that area reaching far beyond the employees of the actual factory. So the so-called 'multiplier effect' is a key concept. We think every student can hold on to Vida Godson's explanation. If you are worried by the mathematics of page 90, express the ideas in words rather than symbols, at least initially. Again we stress that you will not be asked in an examination to remember the formula.

the inputs to an economy which can, to a greater or lesser extent, be manipulated by governments through their control over interest rates and taxes. It is worth noting that governments also try to influence patterns of consumer spending towards the same ends. In this connection one of the most useful theories to be developed has been that of the 'multiplier', which arose out of early work by R. S. Kahn and was developed by J. M. Keynes in his famous treatise, *The General Theory of Employment, Interest and Money*. Keynes dealt only in broad aggregates but nevertheless his reasoning is of relevance to work at other scales and it is worthy of our attention.

The chief importance of Keynes's argument for regional analysis was simply that cycles of growth and decline are self-generating through the mechanism of consumer spending. That is, if a certain amount of income is injected into the economy through investment, consumer spending will rise. In the first instance the amount of this spending will be slightly less than that of the investment because the people receiving the new income created by the investment will tend to save some of it. But the proportion of new income which is spent, say on clothes or washing machines, is passed on and becomes someone else's new income – the tailor, washing machine manufacturer, wholesaler and retailer, will all receive some of the money. Then a proportion of *their* new income is in turn spent on further consumption, and so on through several 'rounds' of spending. Thus the income created from the initial investment in the employment of one group of people is acted upon by a 'multiplier' effect as a proportion of the extra money is repeatedly re-spent, so that the total amount of new income created is very much greater than the amount initially injected into the economy.[1] Keynes used the term 'marginal propensity to consume' to describe the proportion of new income which is spent rather than saved.

The relevance of the multiplier concept for the programming of regional development is clear, but as we have already said, the Keynesian multiplier is a highly aggregated phenomenon which lumps together growth in all sectors of the economy and all parts of the country. The regional analyst requires more detailed information. Primarily he needs to know how much growth will

---

1   The obvious practical value of an understanding of this mechanism led Keynes to observe that, provided one could set a value to the proportion of added income which would be spent, or the marginal propensity to consume, one could estimate the income multiplier and hence the total additional income which would be created as the result of a given investment. His reasoning can be demonstrated quite easily by the manipulation of one simple equation.

Given that: $$Y = C + I$$ where Y = income

C = consumption

I = investment

then $$I = Y - C$$

Isolating Y on the right hand side: $I = Y (1 - C/Y)$

or: $$Y = I \left(\frac{1}{1 - C/Y} \right) *$$

Now from this final equation *, if we know I (the scale of the initial investment) and want to solve for Y (the total income arising from this investment) we need only to estimate the fraction C/Y – the proportion of consumption to income, or marginal propensity to consume – in order to gain a solution. Since spending must always be less than or equal to income, the denominator of the expression in brackets in equation * must always be some number between 0 and 1, so the value of the whole expression $\left(\frac{1}{1 - C/Y} \right)$ must always be greater than 1. Thus Y, the total addition to income, will be greater than the initial investment. The expression $\left(\frac{1}{1 - C/Y} \right)$ is now known as the Keynesian income multiplier. (The fraction C/Y describing the marginal propensity to consume is often replaced by the single letter K or some other letter indicating a constant.)

be included in his particular region in response to an initial investment. In terms of the Keynesian multiplier this requires being able to estimate not just the marginal propensity to consume but the marginal propensity to consume locally (that proportion of new income which will be spent within the local area), for initially it is only that spending which will provide new income and employment for others in the region. (Subsequently, inter-regional feedbacks will come into operation but the effect of these will be much more limited.) The more sophisticated analyst will also want to know which sectors of the economy – heavy industry, consumer durables, services – will receive most impetus from an investment planted in a particular industry, for some sectors of a regional economy may be much more in need of stimulus than others. Thus regional analysts have turned a great deal of their attention to the problem of regional multipliers and have come up with a variety of models ranging in complexity, comprehensiveness and data requirements, which are useful for a range of different situations. The most comprehensive of these are the inter-regional input-output models which will be discussed in the next section, but the simplest regional multipliers are those associated with economic base studies, and it is those which we will start by discussing here.

2.2   The export base model [1]

If one looks at the history of a particular region such as the north-west Pacific coast of the United States or the north-west region of England, one is soon struck by a common feature. In each case the region rose to prosperity at a time when the world demand for its resource endowments was high. In the north-west Pacific coast region it was furs, wheat and timber: in Lancashire it was coal and port facilities. In both these situations national or world demand caused rapid growth in particular export sectors, but closely associated with this came expansion of related industries and service enterprises – flour milling, precision tools, insurance and so on. Tourism on the Yugoslavian coast is just one more of many examples which could be invoked to demonstrate generalized growth of a regional economy as a result of a boom in certain export sectors, for tourism may be counted as an export as it attracts funds from elsewhere. Conversely it is easy to cite examples of regional decline following the collapse of trade in export commodities – Lancashire cotton goods are but one case in point.

Thus it is not surprising that the idea that a region's growth depends on the goods and services (shopping facilities, repair work etc.) which it produces locally but sells beyond its borders is a very old one, for it can easily be argued that these 'basic' activities provide both the means of payment for materials which the region cannot produce itself and the consumer income to support the service activities which are principally local in scope and market area. Depending on the size of region being studied, the terms used to describe the different sorts of activity have variously been export and residentiary, basic and service, basic and non-basic, and further permutations of these dichotomies. The terms export and residentiary are most commonly used when discussing large regions, while basic and non-basic are usually used in the context of city regions where the idea of 'exporting' activities is less meaningful.

Alexander traces the first expression of the idea to Aurousseau in 1921, but

1   Editor's note: You will see that in 2.2 to 2.5 Vida Godson is asking you to look at one indirect way of approaching the regional multiplier idea, based on employment for 'export' beyond the region, or employment to serve the region itself. We think that you will find the basic argument quite clear, and the formulae are in essence quite simple ratios or proportions. You may at first reading find it frustrating that there are continually mentioned difficulties in operating the concept, but Vida Godson explains this in 2.5.

the major early work on the subject was done in the late 1930s by Hoyt whose primary concern was at the level of the city. He attempted to measure a basic non-basic 'ratio', using total employment as his index of the level of activity in each sector. From this data a regional multiplier k can easily be calculated.

$$k = \frac{\text{Total employ. in basic activities} + \text{Total employ. in non-basic activities}}{\text{Total employ. in basic activities}}$$

Increase in employment in basic and non-basic activities is commonly used in place of *total* employment as it is generally considered to yield more relevant results but the type of computation should depend on the purpose of a particular study. You should note that, unlike the multipliers which we discussed in the previous section, this is an *employment* multiplier but it can be used in an exactly analogous fashion to forecast expansion in total employment in response to an anticipated expansion in basic employment. By the use of employment-to-population ratios these forecasts may then be converted to population forecasts if this is thought to be desirable.

Some analysts, however, are more cautious about applying the basic or export multiplier concept and prefer to restrict the use of the basic/non-basic ratio to the more limited purpose of aiding our understanding of the composition of local and regional economies. Certainly the ratio can be quite useful even if restricted to this objective. Alexander particularly advocates its use as an index of a region's 'space-relationships' and sees two main ways in which it may aid our understanding. It clarifies the economic ties of a city or region to other areas, and it enables one to classify areas according to their regional or national function.

2.3 Measurement of the export base

One of the major problems associated with export base models is the purely technical one of measurement. As we have seen, the concept of the export base model is quite straightforward but there are two questions which have to be answered before it can be made operational. First, what unit should one use to measure the level of activity in any particular sector? And second, what criteria should one adopt to distinguish between basic or export activities and residentiary ones?

Indirectly we have already encountered the problem of *selection of an appropriate unit of measurement* in the fact that Hoyt formulated his model in terms of employment. In most countries employment statistics are fairly readily available and in some cases these are in fact the only statistics available. The justification for their use must therefore be paramount in these situations. But a moment's reflection will demonstrate the unreliability of the measure. The employment and spending power generated by a pin factory employing many people may not even equal that of a hydro-electric installation operated by just one or two engineers. The same increases in employment in two industries paying significantly different wages will lead to very different multiplier effects. But conversely little or no change in employment does not necessarily indicate that there has been no expansion in a particular sector, for over a period of years changes in *per capita* productivity can result in quite considerable expansion of a firm's output with no increase in the labour force.

These difficulties can be overcome to some extent by the use of total payrolls as the unit of measurement or by using wage levels as weightings with employment data. Both methods are generally an improvement, particularly if used in conjunction with simple employment data, but they also have their drawbacks for they ignore the influence of unearned income and changes in the general level of prices over time.

The problems associated with the *identification of the basic and service components* are really more fundamental. Several methods have been adopted but again each has its drawbacks. The most straightforward is that of direct survey. But apart from the problems presented by the sheer size of the task, many inaccuracies are likely to arise simply because entrepreneurs do not naturally keep records which distinguish between export and other sales at a regional level and are quite likely to make rather bad estimates of the proportion in each category. It is particularly difficult to make such estimates in cases of non-marketable goods and services such as education. Misallocation of output into the local use category instead of exports is also very likely in cases of indirect export. Many products such as sparking plugs or thermostats are produced only as intermediate goods which are sold almost entirely to other manufacturers. Thus the entire output of a sparking plug factory might be sold to a motor manufacturing concern just down the road and would therefore be likely to be recorded as a local activity, but if the motor manufacturer's cars are sold outside the region the activity of producing sparking plugs should really be looked upon as an exporting one.

It is much more usual to use indirect methods to estimate the size of the export base. These fall into two categories – the ad hoc assumption approach and the Location Quotient (LQ) method. The first merely involves the analyst in making arbitrary assignments of each industry to either the export or local category. The errors of the method can obviously be enormous for, even if one takes a quite fine industrial classification, the vast majority of industries are 'mixed'.

The LQ is the most common method of estimating the export base. This index of specialization has already been discussed quite fully in this course in the correspondence text for Unit 3, pp. 17–18, but to refresh your memory it is defined as follows:

$$LQ_i = \frac{S_i/N_i}{S/N}$$ where LQ_i = The location quotient for industry i in region S

S_i = Number employed in industry i in region S

N_i = Number employed in industry i in the nation

S = Total number employed in all industries in region S

N = Total employed population in the nation

The LQ is therefore an index of 'surplus' or 'deficit' employment in each sector, using the national average as the norm. Use of the LQ as a method of estimating the export base is based on the assumption that local specialization in production implies export of surplus product. Any quotient greater than 1 is taken to indicate the presence of export activity. The size of the base is then calculated by taking, for each industry with a LQ greater than 1, the difference between actual regional employment in that industry and the pro rata share of national employment. The sum across all industries of these surplus employment figures is then taken to represent total basic employment.

Inevitably there are problems associated with the method, primarily that it assumes that local patterns of consumption and productivity are the same as those of the nation in general and that local demand is served entirely by local production, but the drawbacks of this method should not be overstressed for in other respects it has many advantages. In particular it does take account of indirect exports and linked products, it is very cheap and easy to collect and it can be applied to historical data.

2.4 Theoretical limitations of the model

Apart from the largely technical problems which we have mentioned in the previous section there are some rather more fundamental limitations to the export base model. These have been discussed at length by Tiebout (in his article 'Exports and Regional Economic Growth') and Isard (in *Methods of Regional Analysis*) but here we will just mention five points most relevant to this course:

(i) Even as a purely descriptive tool the export-service ratio is a very unstable measure which is highly sensitive to the particular regional boundaries which are chosen. Two extreme examples will demonstrate the degree of variation in the role played by exports in the growth of regions of different sizes. In the simplest case of an exchange economy the wealth of a single person or a small hamlet will depend almost entirely on the extent to which they can produce goods over and above their own requirements. But in an economy such as that of the USA exports account for only a small proportion of national income and in the limiting case the world economy grows entirely on the basis of its members 'taking in each other's washing'. Clearly there is a fallacy somewhere in the reasoning behind the export base model as a predictor of growth and even as a purely descriptive tool great care must be taken in comparing different size regions.

(ii) There is evidence that variables other than exports play a significant role and may be just as autonomous with respect to regional income as are exports. The rates of business investment, government expenditure and residential construction are but three of these.

(iii) In some cases a region's ability to export may depend upon its level of service activity, apparently in direct opposition to the export base theory. Suppose a coalfield were discovered in the Sahara. A decision would have to be made as to whether or not this should be developed. A major factor entering into this decision would have to be the ability of the region to support the residentiary activities required to exploit the mineral. Could enough water, food and building material be found locally to support the mining community at a cost which would make extraction profitable?

(iv) An extension of this paradox exists in cases where a region's prosperity depends in part on feedback from the prosperity of neighbouring regions. In these cases a region A's ability to export to its neighbour B depends on the prosperity of B, which may itself depend on the level of B's sales to A. Thus the level of A's exports will become a function of its imports. This is a familiar paradox in international trade.

(v) Even if one were to ignore the three preceding problems and were prepared to assume that for certain medium sized regions exports probably were the most significant consideration and could be thought of as largely autonomous, projections based on the export base multiplier would be likely to result in some inaccuracies. Use of the multiplier involves two major assumptions concerning the stability of productive practices. It requires that there are no changes in productivity during the projection period and that there are no changes in the technology of either production or transportation which would result in changes in the regional pattern of trade. It is possible that these assumptions could be upheld through short projection but the nature of the multiplier, which relies on the response of service employment to increased basic employment, essentially requires that it be allowed a fairly long period to work itself out. Finally in this vein, the constant nature of the export base coefficient also hides the fact that it is only an aggregative coefficient describing the relationship between export and residentiary employment. Thus we have no right to expect that it will give an accurate indication of the amount of service employment likely to result from specific increases in employment in basic industries as diverse as coal mining and aerospace research.

2.5 Justification for using the export base model

You may by now be wondering why we have devoted time to examining the export base model if it is so unreliable. But justification is easy not only on pedagogic and historical grounds but also on practical ones. On the one hand the model, despite all these drawbacks, is a useful quick, crude measure applicable in an area in which all techniques seem fraught with technical and theoretical limitations. On the other hand, this thorough examination of a rather simplistic model enables us to clarify our ideas on what we really need from a regional multiplier model and how we might set about satisfying these requirements. The inter-regional input-output model is probably the best such model to date and we will devote the next section to examining it in some detail.

3 Input-output models[1]

3.1 Economic interdependence and flows

We have noted that two of the most serious problems associated with export base multipliers are that they do not take account of intermediate or linked products and that they are too aggregated – they employ just one coefficient to describe the relationship between numerous export and service sectors. The input-output model permits us to overcome both of these problems, for at its most basic it is nothing more than a table recording the flows of goods and services from each sector of the economy to every other and to final consumption. It thus aims explicitly to describe the structure of the economy in such a way as to demonstrate each link in the chain of inter-dependence between activities. It is essentially an empirical description of the economy.

The inter-industry linkages which can be described in a table recording all the flows of goods and services between sectors are of great interest to the economic analyst, for the effect of one industry employing the output of other industries as its raw materials has many repercussions. If there is expansion in one sector, such as the shipbuilding industry, there will be an increase in the demand for all the products – furniture, boilers, plastic flowers, paint – which are supplied to fit out the ships. Any other industries supplying the furniture and paint firms will also subsequently feel the effects of the increased demand. Thus the initial expansion in shipbuilding is passed on through 'rounds of expansion' in a fashion very similar to that described by

---

1 Editor's note: You may feel at about this point that we are asking you to look back again at economic geography, or even at economics. But this series of tools are precisely those lacking to Professor Learmonth and his team in Mysore in 1956–8 (see television programme and paragraph 4.2 in Section A of this unit). To go back for a moment to our new factory making calculating machines (see editor's note on 2.1 above) it is familiar enough that this will increase electric power demands, use engineering components, food for its canteen and so on. It may come as a surprise to you that one can think of a kind of book-keeping exercise about how an industry affects other industries. The idea is exciting and valuable, and in our experience very few students have great difficulties with it. The main thing is not to be afraid of tabulations like that on p. 102. And the simple formulas on pp. 97–8 can be tackled first using words instead of symbols if you are not used to these, for the key to the symbols is given. Again concentrate on the relationships the formula brings out, rather than try to memorize it. Do not be put off by Section 3.3 on applications and 3.4 on limitations which still do not feed back to the kind of regional problem you think a geographer might be involved in. Section 3.5 will bring this to you.

Keynes in the context of consumer spending. The only difference is that it is the demand for intermediate goods which results in the inter-industry multiplier whereas Keynes referred only to final demand.

An interest in economic inter-dependence appears to date back at least to 1758 when Francois Quesnay published his 'Tableau Economique'. The original table depicted the operation of a single establishment, a farm, but later Quesnay published a modified version of the Tableau in which he tried to represent the entire economy of his day. Further development of the idea, however, waited for over a century until 1874 when Léon Walras published his 'Éléments d'économie politique pure'. Walras presented a system of equations which introduced the notion of coefficients of production but he was primarily interested in the simultaneous determination of prices in the system and as he pre-dated computers and lacked much essential data, he considered his system a purely theoretical model, for the computations required to implement it presented insurmountable problems. Thus the culmination of the work started by Quesnay waited until the 1930s when Professor Wassily Leontief of Harvard University was able to complete the model and give it empirical content as a result of the development of electronic computers.

Leontief's original tables referred to the United States economy and as the modifications required to adapt the input-output model for regional use make it slightly more complicated we will describe the form of the most straight-forward national table first.

3.2 The Leontief input-output model

The basis of Leontief's input-output model is the transactions table. A hypothetical transactions table is presented in Table 1. There are three major parts to this table which we will deal with separately – the processing sector, the final demand and payments sectors, and the total input and output row and column. The processing sector is the most fundamental and we will start with that. This is the block of rows (running across the table) and columns (running down the table) appearing in the top left hand corner of the figure. Within it are recorded the values of transactions of goods and services (it is

Table 1
Hypothetical transactions table (after Miernyk)

From \ To	Industry 1	Industry 2	Industry 3	...	Industry J	....	Industry n	House holds		Export		Total Value of Outputs
Industry 1	x_{11}	x_{12}	x_{13}				x_{1n}		y_1			$x_{1.}$
Industry 2	x_{21}	x_{22}					x_{2n}		y_2			x_2
Industry 3	x_{31}											
⋮												
Industry i					x_{ij}							
⋮												
Industry n	x_{n1}	x_{n2}	x_{n3}				x_{nn}		y_n			
Labour												
Imports												
Total Value of Inputs	x_1	x_2										

customary to use producers' prices) which pass from the sectors listed down the left hand side (LHS) of the table to those labelled across the top. We have represented only a few sectors here in a schematic manner because that is all that space allows but a real table may include anything from 50 to about 200 different sectors, depending on the purpose of the model and the capacity of the computer on which it is to be run. The small figures x_{11}, x_{12} etc. which have been inserted in this part of the table represent the value of the transactions from the industries enumerated by the first subscript (listed down the LHS of the table) to those with the second subscript (across the top of the table). Thus the figure x_{ij} gives one the value of the goods sold by the ith industry, perhaps coal, to the jth industry, steel.

The final demand sector is very similar except that it records the value of goods and services going from each sector on the LHS of the table to final consumption. For simplicity final demand may be thought of as households but we have drawn in dashed columns to indicate that it should be sub-divided to distinguish at least government purchases, inventory accumulation (holdings of reserve stocks of goods) and exports to foreign countries. Likewise the payments sector running across the bottom of the table should be disaggregated to distinguish inputs from households (in the form of labour), gross inventory depletion, taxes paid to governments and imports.

The final row and column represent the sums across the preceding rows and columns respectively. That is, the figures in the final row show the total value of all inputs to each sector and those in the final column show the total value of goods distributed to all uses from each sector. The total values of inputs and outputs for each row and column entering into the processing sector should be identical. Those for individual rows and columns in the payments and final demand sectors may not balance exactly but the sectors will balance overall. Thus there will be a unique value in the bottom right hand cell which is both the sum down the final column and across the bottom row. This will represent the total value of inputs to or outputs from the economy, but it should be stressed that this is not the same as the Gross National Product (GNP). In the input-output table there is deliberate and repeated double counting – our sparking plug will be counted once when it is sold to the car manufacturers and again when their car is sold to the consumer – whereas a GNP calculation carefully avoids including the value of any product more than once.

From the information presented in the table it is easy to derive a set of equations describing the productive relationships within the economy. These are usually written in the form of a set of 'final demand equations' in which the final demand values Y_i are written in terms of the other values in each row.

$$Y_1 = X_1 - x_{11} - x_{12} - \ldots\ldots\ldots\ldots\ldots\ldots - x_{1n}$$
$$Y_2 = X_2 - x_{21} - x_{22} - \ldots\ldots\ldots\ldots\ldots\ldots - x_{2n}$$
$$\vdots$$
$$Y_n = X_n - x_{n1} - x_{n2} - \ldots\ldots\ldots\ldots\ldots\ldots - x_{nn}$$

Each equation states that final demand for industry i equals the total output X_i less the amount of i sold to each of the productive sectors, x_{ij}. For our sparking plug manufacturer this means that the amount going to retailers for sale to private consumers will be the total amount manufactured less that sold to manufacturers of cars, aircraft, tractors and so on. The equations may be written in a more general form if we replace each term x_{ij} by the expression

$a_{ij}X_j$ where $a_{ij} = x_{ij}/X_j$. The purpose of this can be explained if we examine the meaning of the fraction x_{ij}/X_j. If x_{ij} represents £50 worth of coal going to the steel industry and X_j represents £250, the total value of steel inputs (or outputs), then $x_{ij}/X_j = a_{ij} = £0\cdot20$, represents *the requirement of coal necessary to produce one pound's worth of steel.*

If $a_{ij} = x_{ij}/X_j$ as we have defined it, it does not alter our equations if we

replace x_{ij} by $a_{ij}X_j$ for by substitution $a_{ij}X_j = \dfrac{x_{ij}}{X_j} X_j$ which, by cancelling the

X_j, is simply x_{ij}.

A new table can now be drawn up for the processing sector showing instead of gross values of transactions, x_{ij}, the per unit output coefficients a_{ij} which describe the technical relationships between all the industries *regardless of the actual volume of output X_j at any one time.* The final demand equations now appear as:

$$Y_1 = X_1 - a_{11}X_1 - a_{12}X_2 - \ldots\ldots\ldots\ldots\ldots - a_{1n}X_n$$
$$Y_2 = X_2 - a_{21}X_1 - a_{22}X_2 - \ldots\ldots\ldots\ldots\ldots - a_{2n}X_n$$

$$\vdots$$

$$Y_n = X_n - a_{n1}X_1 - a_{n2}X_2 - \ldots\ldots\ldots\ldots\ldots - a_{nn}X_n$$

If we assume that the technical coefficients a_{ij} remain constant over moderate periods of time after we have collected the data from which they were calculated, we can use this set of equations to predict the volume of output required from each sector. Suppose one can obtain forecasts for one or all of the final demand sectors Y_i, one can then calculate the total output X_i required from each sector to meet these demands because we have n equations and want to solve these for exactly n unknown values X_1 to X_n. Forecasting of total output requirements in this way clearly has abundant applications and we will discuss some of these in general terms now before going on to describe regional and inter-regional versions of the model.

3.3 Applications of input-output models

As in the case of export base models, if the input-output table were useful for nothing else it would provide an invaluable description of the *structural interdependence of the economy* and would be useful as such to analysts and policy makers. The input-output table is inherently analytical so merely by looking at the size and distribution of the a_{ij} coefficients it is possible to identify parts of the economy which have strong or weak linkages. Comparison of input-output tables for developed and underdeveloped countries can indicate not only that the former have a much greater degree of concentration in the secondary and tertiary sectors but also that they have proportionally many more inter-industry transactions: the developed economy embodies a dense and highly complex network of linkages. Polythene, for example, must be used in almost every sector of the American economy as it is employed in goods ranging from fertilizer bags to glossy file covers and typewriter parts. In contrast the underdeveloped economy typically relies on exports of primary products or on simple one stage manufacturing operations. Development in these countries may mean restructuring the economy so that activity is concentrated in sectors with strong linkages. The input-output table would allow one to select these with some precision.

Once this initial appraisal of the economy has been made it is then possible to use the full power of the input-output model in the direction of multiplier analysis. This will generally take one of two forms – impact analysis or sensitivity checking. *Impact analysis* involves forecasting a specific increase in demand in a particular sector, such as the aerospace industry, building construction or plastics, and calculating the total increase in output in each sector which will be required to meet this new demand. This projection can then be converted into employment figures. There are many examples of impact studies of this sort, notably Isard and Kuenne's study at a regional level of the total employment likely to arise in the Greater New York-Philadelphia region as the result of an expansion of the steel industry in the area. Moore and Peterson did a more general study in Utah computing employment multipliers for each industry in response to estimated increases in demand in a number of sectors.

Sensitivity analysis is effectively an extension of impact analysis whereby, through repeated trials of alternative growth patterns, the analyst seeks to determine which sectors of the economy are most sensitive to certain proposals and which plans result in the most desirable effects in particular, usually depressed, industries. Closely allied to sensitivity studies are various kinds of *feasibility tests*. A question might be raised, for example, about the feasibility of achieving a certain level of employment by a given target date. Or it may seem necessary to check that sufficient resources will be available to achieve the product-mix required to meet a projected level of final demand. If the resources are not available what implications will this have for international trade?

The applications which we have discussed so far have all assumed that the planner is in a position to play a fairly active role in reshaping, directing or controlling the economy. Indeed in the 1950s the use of input-output analysis became somewhat controversial because an impression was created in some quarters that it implied push-button planning and represented a threat to private enterprise. The United States government even withheld funds from input-output studies for some years. But the use of the technique in France demonstrates that this need not be so. French planners have for some time now relied quite heavily on input-output analysis as one of the keystones behind their notion of 'indicative' or *non-coercive planning*. Under this system the French government does not establish production targets or allocate resources and incomes according to some central plan, but leaves these to be worked out largely by the market mechanism. What does happen is that the French Planning Commission, using an input-output model, makes detailed projections of final demand and total output by sectors for a specified future period. These projections provide entrepreneurs with a very useful set of production targets, for although skilled managers usually know a fair amount about any changes which are likely to affect their markets directly, it is rare that they have the ability to forecast both direct and indirect requirements for their commodity with any certainty. By indicating production targets in this manner the French government enables businessmen to organize their concerns so that they can operate economically and at full capacity.

3.4   Limitations of the basic input-output model

Many of the problems associated with input-output models are similar to those which we discussed in connection with export base models for they stem from a common feature. Although the input-output model is a vast improvement on the simple export base model because it disaggregates the economy and takes account of intermediate products, it nevertheless still relies for its dynamic projections on *constant coefficients* describing the static structure of the economy at one point in time. In the export base model the basic-service ratio is assumed to hold constant: in the input-output model it is the entire table of technical coefficients, a_{ij}. This means that the input-output model assumes two things about the nature of production. First, it assumes that there is *no substitution between inputs* in any industry. If coal is the source of power to the steel industry in the base year it must still be used at the end of the projection period. This implies that the model is incapable of taking into account either technological improvements or changes in relative price levels. Second, the constant coefficient assumption implies that all productive processes have *constant returns to scale*. That is, the same value of inputs is required to produce each unit of output regardless of whether the factory is producing three cars a day or three hundred. The indivisibility of many inputs, particularly labour and machinery, usually causes increasing returns to scale but decreasing returns can also occur if a plant is overstrained. (You will remember that we have already discussed economies of scale in some detail in Unit 6.) If increasing returns operate in a particular sector the input-output model will over-estimate the amount of inputs required to satisfy increased final or intermediate demands.

A problem of a similar nature deriving from the need to limit the model to a finite number of technical coefficients is that *aggregation of dissimilar sectors* is inevitable. The extent to which this occurs will of course depend on the resources available and the size of the model, but even a model which differentiates as many as 200 sectors has to do a great deal of compression for one could distinguish many thousands of different enterprises. The only entirely satisfactory classification would be one which differentiated between inputs at the level of individual products and firms. This is clearly quite impossible and it is necessary to use coefficients which relate to input proportions of entire industries. The input-output model must give an inaccurate estimate of the input requirements associated with a forecast increased demand for say chemicals, unless coincidentally that demand happens to be evenly distributed between all the products of the chemical industry.

Still in a similar vein is the problem associated with the fact that the a_{ij} coefficients which appear in the table are usually *average coefficients* representing the pattern of production in 'average' firms in the industry. If the forecasting period is fairly long it is likely that the technologically most advanced businesses will survive best and that very old fashioned firms will either die or change their practices. Thus the use of average coefficients for projection will tend to give a somewhat historic picture. In fact some input-output studies try to overcome this problem by using a_{ij} coefficients calculated from 'best practice' firms. An extension of this problem is that associated with the emergence of entirely *new industries* during the projection period. If it is suspected that an industry which has already appeared elsewhere may be transferred into the area under study, it can be budgeted for by borrowing a row and column of coefficients from the input-output table of the nation where it is already established. The development of a domestic computer industry in South America, for example, could be handled in this way. But the emergence of an entirely new and unforeseen industry is, of course, impossible to budget for.

Finally, projection errors may arise from the fact that there may be insufficient industrial capacity to meet requirements forecast by the model. The model in fact assumes that there is sufficient *excess capacity* and *unemployment* to allow one to meet any possible distribution of future output requirements. This is seldom true. In particular labour can very rarely be treated as an undifferentiated commodity and it is most unusual for capital to be available in unlimited quantities. It is well known that two problems which hamper the development of many countries more than almost any others are lack of capital and lack of skilled labour for even though these problems can usually be surmounted in the long term, it takes a considerable time to build new plant and machinery and to re-deploy and train labour.

Problems of data collection are virtually self-evident but in practice rarely prove insurmountable. By 1965 input-output tables had been prepared for over 40 national economies ranging from the United States, France and the United Kingdom to a number of underdeveloped nations. The tool can to some extent be tailored to the resources available but the development of a table does require stable central financing and organization.

3.5   Regional and inter-regional models [1]

'It is not too much of an overstatement to say that post-World War II regional research has been almost completely dominated by regional applications of input-output models' (Tiebout, 1957). This statement is still essentially true today.

The regional input-output model is in essence nothing more than the national model applied to a small area, but the construction of models for sub-national units does raise two types of problem. The first is essentially an operational one – that of obtaining data at this level. The second is more fundamental, arising out of the fact that regional economies tend to be much more 'open' than national ones. That is, exports and imports between regions tend to form a much larger proportion of total transactions.

Two sorts of method exist for overcoming the data problem. The most obvious is of course *direct survey* but this is subject to all the difficulties of expense and inaccurate estimation which we have already discussed in other contexts. The other method is to use *adjusted national coefficients*. The rationale for this is that in cases of very large or heterogeneous regions the use of national coefficients may give a reasonable approximation of regional input patterns because the industrial structure of such a region may reflect quite closely the average for the nation. But in most regions the input patterns differ quite significantly from the national average as local resources or products are used preferentially. The use of coal in the East Midlands would be an example of this. The patterns of inputs in a region tend always to be biased in favour of the use of local products in any cases where a degree of input substitution is permissible. It has, therefore, seemed reasonable to analysts to use indices of regional concentration in each sector as weights on national input coefficients. The weighting index most commonly used is a modified Location Quotient – an inter-industry location quotient, LQ_{ij}, which describes the relative regional concentrations of industries i and j.

$$LQ_{ij} = \frac{RE_i/RE_j}{NE_i/NE_j} \text{ where } RE_i = \text{ Regional employment in industry } i$$

$$NE_i = \text{ National employment in industry } i$$

If LQ_{ij} is less than one ($LQ_{ij} < 1$) the technical coefficient for region R, a_{ij}^R, is calculated by using LQ_{ij} to weight down the national coefficient a_{ij}.

$$a_{ij}^R = LQ_{ij} \, a_{ij} \qquad \text{for all } LQ_{ij} < 1$$

That is, if any industry is under-represented in the region under study the national input coefficient is scaled down. But if LQ_{ij} is greater than or equal to one ($LQ_{ij} \geqslant 1$) the national coefficient is used unadjusted. This convention is adopted because if the a_{ij} were scaled up one could easily get regional coefficients so large that $\Sigma_i a_{ij}^R > 1$. That would mean that the value of the sum of all the

---

1   Editor's note: You are now asked to apply the idea of 'book-keeping between industries' to 'book keeping within regions' and 'book-keeping between regions'. Assuming regional planning of some kind, you probably do not need to be convinced of the value of the approach. Do try to hold on to the main argument even if you are initially unhappy with the various formulae used. Again concentrate on the relationships studied by feeding in words from the key to symbols, at least until you are familiar with the use of formulae.

inputs i going to produce j would be greater than the total value of X_j produced!

The problems raised by the relative *openness of regional economies* are more difficult to get around. The national input-output model only records foreign trade in the payments and final demand sectors. Imports and exports in all industries are lumped together into a single row and column and as they appear as part of the dependent variable (on the LHS of the equality sign) in the system of final demand equations they do not enter into the problem when direct and indirect requirements for each sector X_i are calculated. Only those industries in the endogenous or internal processing sector are included in this computation. Thus any multiplier effects arising from transactions with industries outside the region are ignored. The significance of this omission will depend on the size and autonomy of the region. If regional exports and imports are thought to play a very significant role a special table is sometimes constructed so that it is possible to examine the export and import coefficients disaggregated by industry. The limitations of this sort of table, however, lead us directly into the topic of inter-regional models.

Inter-regional (or multi-regional) models are effectively the outcome of integrating a number of models for different regions. The result is a huge square table divided into a number of sub-tables as shown in Table 2. The tables which

Table 2
Hypothetical inter-regional transactions table

From \ To			NORTH			MIDLANDS			SOUTH	
		Industry 1	Industry 2	....	Industry 1	Industry 2	....	Industry 1	Industry 2	....
NORTH	Industry 1									
	Industry 2									
	⋮			NN xij			NM xij			NS xij	
MIDLANDS	Industry 1									
	Industry 2									
	⋮						MM xij			
SOUTH	Industry 1									
	Industry 2									
	⋮			SN xij						SS xij	

$\begin{smallmatrix}SN\\xij\end{smallmatrix}$ represents the value of goods sent from industry in region S to industry j in region N

$\begin{smallmatrix}NN\\xij\end{smallmatrix}$ represents the value of goods sent from industry i to industry j within region N

lie along the main diagonal of this 'super-table' describe the internal transactions of each region, while the off-diagonal blocks give a complete description of all inter-regional transactions. The element x_{ij}^{RS} thus gives the value of goods sent from industry i in region R to industry j in region S. As this table is square it generates a set of simultaneous equations with as many unknowns as equations, which is consequently soluble. It is, therefore, possible to calculate from this model the output required from industry i in region R to satisfy an increased demand Y_j^S for industry j in region S, and all the direct and indirect requirements for the product generated by inter-regional feedbacks are fully accounted for. The main uses of the model are for regional balance of payments studies and inter-regional flow studies, for determining regional implications of national projections and national implications of regional projections.[1]

The tremendous added power of the full inter-regional model is not, however, obtained without penalty, for by laying out the inter-regional flow coefficients in full we impose even more stringent *stability conditions*. In the national model the condition of constant input coefficients a_{ij} meant that we were assuming that no substitution between inputs was possible and that there were constant returns to scale. The condition that a_{ij}^{RS} must be constant in the inter-regional model specifies not only that the amount of a particular input per unit of output is constant but also its regional source. That is, trading patterns and relative prices in different regions are assumed to be stable. Similarly the *excess capacity assumptions* of the national model are more stringent in the inter-regional case. There must be both excess industrial capacity and labour in each region and excess transport capacity between every pair of regions.

An interesting extension of regional and inter-regional input-output studies lies in consideration of the relationship between input-output multipliers, regional impact studies and the location theorist's model of industrial *agglomeration*, for one of the most prevalent themes in regional planning in the last ten years has been the subject of 'growth poles' and their potential for regional development. There has been much confusion over what precisely regional planners have in mind when they use the term 'growth pole' but one definition which has been agreed by some research workers in the field runs as follows: 'A growth pole is an urban centre of economic activity which can achieve self-sustaining growth to the point that growth is diffused outward into the pole region and eventually beyond into the less developed region of the nation.' Regional planners have imagined that it is possible to create these growth poles artificially by injecting a certain amount of capital into key industries in a regional centre. The combined processes of inter-industry multipliers and agglomeration tendencies are expected to come into operation virtually automatically so that the initial investment attracts spatially concentrated expansion in related sectors of the economy. Subsequently, when the pole itself has attained self-sustaining growth, the influence of this thriving micro-economy is expected to spread to more remote parts of the region. Actual applications of the inter-regional input-output model, however, demonstrate that it is not uncommon for a large proportion of the multiplier

---

1 The problem of obtaining data, particularly for the off-diagonal sub-tables is handled by a technique similar to that used for adjusting national coefficients for simple regional models. The technique was put forward by Leon Moses and depends on combining inter-regional trade data with inter-industry input data in the following way:

$$x_{ij}^{RS} = t_i^{RS} x_{ij}^S$$

where x_{ij}^{RS} = value of goods sent from industry i in region R to industry j in region S

      t_i^{RS} = value of goods of type i sent from region R to region S

      x_{ij}^S = value of inputs from industry i to industry j in region S

The advantage of this technique is that the two pieces of information x_{ij}^S and t_i^{RS} are both comparatively easily available whereas the inter-regional disaggregation x_{ij}^{RS} is virtually unobtainable.

effect attendant on an investment to accrue beyond the boundaries of the region in which it was initially planted. If this is so we have no right to expect that concentrated investment will automatically generate regional growth and the prominent position which growth pole ideas hold in regional planning makes investigation of this relationship between spatial concentration and investment multipliers a matter for urgent consideration.

4 Allocation problems and linear programming

4.1 Allocation problems and planning [1]

At the heart of almost all planning problems, whether they be at a national, regional or institutional level, lies the problem of finding the 'best' allocation of resources or benefits amongst a set of alternatives. It may be a question of the distribution of scarce inputs amongst alternative uses or one of distribution of commodities (or some other benefit such as accessibility to schools, clinics, shops or transport facilities) amongst consumers. The problem is to achieve the distribution in such a way as to maximize some quantity such as *per capita* income, employment or profit, or to minimize total cost, travel time or land devoted to a particular purpose.

In all these situations the problem has a similar form with two distinct aspects. The first characteristic is that there is always some objective to which one is seeking an optimal solution. The second is that the allocation must always meet with certain constraints or side conditions – the demands on scarce resources cannot exceed the amount of these resources available, or certain minimum requirements must be satisfied in some way. It is the existence of these constraints which makes each problem one of allocation or distribution, for without them the problem of optimization would be trivial. It is only if we cannot have more guns without having less butter that any choice is necessary.

The sort of problem which confronts the regional planner particularly frequently is that of finding an optimal mix of industries for a region which will maximize gross regional product (GRP) subject to the constraint that the number of tasks to which the region's resources can be devoted is limited. Another typical problem is one of minimizing the cost of carrying out a regional programme such as providing health facilities, subject to the constraints of certain minimum standards. In either problem there are many different ways in which the constraints can be satisfied. There would be thousands of different combinations of industrial production which would be permissible within the constraints of the resources available in the region, or innumerable hospital and clinic arrangements which would satisfy basic medical standards. But in each case there will only be one solution which will also satisfy the main objective to maximize GRP or minimize the cost of medical provision.

These allocation problems have always been with us but various factors combine to make them more important in modern society than ever before. On the one hand, population pressure and increasing affluence make greater and greater demands on our scarce resources. Among the most notable

1 Editor's note: Students able to watch the television programme related to this unit may find some help there in approaching this problem – and the television notes and relevant off-print material may help too. However, we think that Vida Godson's treatment, simple example, and exercise (in the supplementary material for this unit) make an excellent step-by-step introduction to this technique. You may not all be able to solve complex real-world problems using linear programming, but we think that every student not afraid of graphs and simple formulas can appreciate the principles involved in using this tool in deciding which combination of resources in a region should be used to further a chosen objective like increasing employment or income as much as the resource limitations permit.

examples of resources which are now under severe strain because of this are, of course, open space, hydro-carbon fuels and pure water. On the other hand, constantly improving technology is always widening the range of uses to which resources can be put. Thus the choices open to decision makers become more and more complex and it becomes extremely important that we should find new techniques of analysis which will enable us to make better decisions, weighing the relative importance of all these possible combinations of solutions. The well established field of differential calculus enables us to handle many sorts of optimization problems but fails on problems where the constraints set only upper or lower limits to be satisfied. But necessity is the mother of invention and the last 25 years have seen the development of a family of techniques, known collectively as mathematical programming, which are designed specifically to cope with problems of this sort.

4.2   Linear programming

The family of mathematical programming techniques includes all problems which have the general form of requiring that some function be optimized (maximized or minimized) subject to a set of constraints. Within the family different sorts of programming are differentiated according to the nature of the objective function (see below), the form of the constraints or the structure of the set of feasible solutions.

The simplest, best developed and consequently most frequently used branch of the family is linear programming, so called because in this class of problem both the objective and the constraints are represented by linear functions. (A linear function describing the relationship between one variable Y and one or more others X_1 X_2 etc., is one which can be written as a simple equation of the form $Y = a + b_1 X_1 + b_2 X_2$, where a, b_1 and b_2 are all constants. This sort of equation can be represented by a straight line or plane if described graphically. Any function which includes higher powers of X_1 and X_2 or more complex relations between X_1 and X_2, such as $Y = a(X_1)^2/(X_2)^3$, is non-linear.) Some of the other branches of the programming family are non-linear programming which may have either a non-linear objective function or non-linear constraints, integer programming which includes as one of the constraints the condition that the solution must be an integer or whole number, and dynamic programming where an optimal programme of decisions is calculated for a sequence of discrete time periods. Integer programming is particularly useful for certain types of planning problems where fractional solutions, such as a recommendation to build $2\frac{1}{2}$ dams, are meaningless, but we must limit ourselves here to describing only the simplest sorts of programme – the linear type. (In the television programme accompanying this unit Professor Learmonth also discusses a linear programming problem and it will be useful for you to look over that material in addition to this section.)

Linear programming was first developed by George Danzig in 1947 as a technique for planning diversified activities for the US Air Force. As it is not possible to find an optimal solution to a problem of this sort analytically, Danzig developed a method for searching amongst all the possible solutions which satisfy the constraints to find the optimal solution in the least number of steps. It is possible to describe Danzig's formulation of the problem both graphically and in equation form. Of course all realistic problems have to be solved algebraically using high speed computers but a toy example can be solved using a diagram.

Suppose we were a regional planning authority faced with the problem of making an investment so as to maximize the addition to gross regional product (GRP) in part of Scotland. We want to decide what combination of industry and agriculture we should support to bring about this objective given that the region has limited supplies of skilled labour and that we have limited capital to invest. (We shall restrict ourselves to just two activities and two constraints in order to keep the problem to one which can easily be solved diagramatically. In a real problem we could handle 20 or more sub-divisions of industry and agriculture and as many constraints without difficulty.) We know that the return (net profit) on industrial output is say £10(000) per unit per annum and that on agriculture is £8(000) per unit. (A 'unit' could be thought of as a factory or farm of a certain size or any other element of production which would be useful as a decision tool.) Thus we can write down our objective to maximize GRP as follows:

Maximize $GRP = 10X + 8A$ where X = number of units of industrial production to be supported

A = number of units of agricultural production to be supported

This equation, which is known as the *objective function*, enables one to calculate the total return to be expected from any combination of industrial and agricultural production because the number of units of each sort is multiplied by the profit per unit on that type of production. Thus if the regional planning authority decided to back 3 factories and 2 modern farming units the addition to GRP would be $10(3) + 8(2) = £46(000)$.

In order to express the *constraints* mathematically we need to know the requirements made on skilled labour and capital by both industrial and agricultural production. Suppose we have £120(000) worth of capital available and a skilled labour force of 3(000) men. Industrial production of the sort envisaged requires 500 skilled workers per unit while agriculture only requires 100, but agricultural units need £20(000) of capital and industrial ones only £10(000). Our constraints can, therefore, be expressed as follows:

$0·5X + 0·1A \leqslant 3$ (available skilled labour in thousands)

$10·0X + 20·0A \leqslant 120$ (available capital in £1000s)

The first expression tells us that the amount of skilled labour used in industrial production and farming must be less than or equal to the 3,000 men available and the second tells us that the amount of capital spent must be less than or equal to £120,000. There are also two other constraints on the problem which need hardly be mentioned verbally because they sound so obvious but must be included in the mathematical expression of the problem to prevent absurd solutions. They are that the numbers of industrial and agricultural units to be supported must be non-negative. The meaning of this will be clearer when we have looked at the problem diagrammatically.

Putting all this information together we can now express the regional planning authority's problem as follows:

Maximize $GRP = 10X + 8A$

Subject to $0·5X + 0·1A \leqslant 3$

$10·0X + 20·0A \leqslant 120$

$X \geqslant 0,   A \geqslant 0$

To solve the problem graphically we must now transfer this information onto a diagram. To start with we need one axis for each variable in the problem, which in this case means we have a two-dimensional diagram in which we represent the number of agricultural units along the horizontal axis and the number of industrial units along the vertical axis. Figure 1 shows the diagrammatic representation of the problem. On this diagram we can then draw in the upper limits of each of the 2 constraints. At the upper limits each expression is met by an equality and since these are linear equations straight lines can be drawn joining all the points (combinations of X and A)

Figure 1
Diagrammatic representation of the linear programming problem

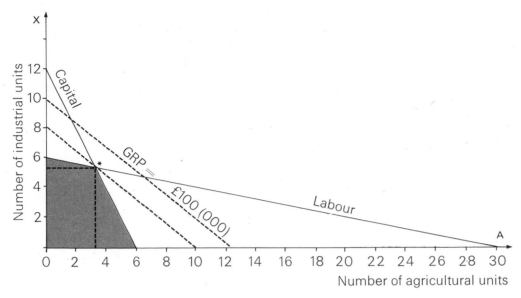

which satisfy each equation. Taking the labour constraint first, we could use up all the labour available by supporting just 30 agricultural units $\left(\dfrac{3.0}{0.1}\right)$ or alternatively we could use it all up with just 6 factories $\left(\dfrac{3.0}{0.5}\right)$. These two facts allow us to mark off the two points at which the equation cuts the axes of our diagram, and as we know that the equation is a straight line, we can draw a line connecting these points which will represent the upper limit of the labour constraint. Similarly if we have no factories we could invest all our capital in 6 farms, and if we have no farms we can have 12 factories. The line joining the points $A = 6$, $X = 0$ and $X = 12$, $A = 0$ represents all the combinations of factories and farms which we could have if we used up all our capital.

These two lines represent the upper limits so all the points lying below and to the left of each line represent combinations of factories and farms which satisfy each constraint, but any points above and to the right of either line violate that constraint. The significance of the two subsidiary constraints, $X \geqslant 0$ and $A \geqslant 0$, can now also be seen for these limit us to examining only those points which lie above the A axis and to the right of the X axis. The combination of all four constraints restricts the possible solution to the problem to those points which lie within the area shaded on the diagram for only these points (combinations of X and A) satisfy all the necessary conditions. This area is known as the *feasible region*.

To solve our problem we want now to select one point from amongst those in the feasible region which will give us the maximum value for our objective function. We can find this point on the diagram if we also draw in a number of lines representing possible positions of the objective function. This equation is not precisely determined for we do not yet know the value of GRP at the maximum, but the slope of the equation is uniquely defined by the ratio of the two constant coefficients. Suppose we allow GRP to take an arbitrary value of 100 so that $100 = 10X + 8A$, then if $X = 0$, $A = 12\frac{1}{2}$ and if $A = 0$, $X = 10$. A dotted line has been drawn to represent the position of the objective function for this value. From the diagram we can see that this GRP is clearly unobtainable for no point on the line passes inside the feasible region. But a whole family of parallel lines could be drawn representing different values of the objective function and we can see that the value of the objective function will rise as the dotted line is pushed upward and to the right. Thus if we want to find a solution which satisfies the two constraints and maximizes the objective function we want to find that point on the edge of the feasible region which lies on the farthest possible objective function away from the origin. In our diagram this must be the point marked by an asterisk. One can now determine the solution to the problem simply by reading off the value of this point against the two axes. Unfortunately the numbers we have chosen in this crude example give us the solution that we should support $3\frac{1}{3}$ farms and $5\frac{1}{3}$ factory units. Factories are not always indivisible units and it might be possible to install smaller factories so we will assume for the moment that this is not an absurd solution but it does rather demonstrate the advantages of the more complex formulation which ensures integer solutions. The net addition to GRP resulting from this investment programme can be calculated by substituting the values for X and A into the objective function.

$$GRP = 10(5 \cdot 333) + 8(3 \cdot 333) \quad \text{(thousand pounds)}$$
$$= \pounds 53,333 + \pounds 26,664$$
$$\simeq \pounds 80,000$$

4.3 The value and limitations of programming models

The value of linear programming can only be demonstrated *in principle* from the description of an unrealistic example such as that which we have just worked through. But with skill and experience it is possible to build much more realistic models. In our example the regional planning authority's investment strategy demonstrated the way in which a linear programming model can be used as a prescriptive tool and indeed this is probably the most attractive quality of the whole family of programming models. Their use, however, should not be thought to be restricted to problems of that sort for their concern with determining optimal solutions means that they are well suited to describe and analyse many sorts of rational (optimizing) behaviour. They have, for example, been used to demonstrate certain properties of the housing market and of travel patterns. In cases such as these it has been thought not unreasonable to assume that the majority of people behave 'rationally' in relation to some objective such as minimizing their travel time.

The drawbacks of linear programming models are, however, fairly obvious. Although by using computers we can include very large numbers of variables and constraints, it is difficult to set down all the possible considerations and alternatives which an experienced decision maker will include in his intuitive calculations. The housewife going shopping is probably the most notorious discriminator. She will weigh price differences against the distance to be travelled, congestion, parking facilities for the pram, her relationship with the butcher and a thousand more subtle benefits and side conditions. Even the best laid programming model could never take account of all these, doubtless entirely 'rational', considerations. Technical problems of measuring many types of constraints and objectives, particularly those of a political nature, also create difficulties, but analysts have shown remarkable dexterity in finding surrogate or substitute measures to replace these elusive ideas.

The limitations associated with the linearity assumptions of the majority of operational programming models are those which have aroused the greatest interest amongst critics, but the matter of whether or not they are justified depends firstly on the nature of the behaviour being modelled and secondly on the purpose of the model building exercise. In the many cases where linear programming models are used to describe productive processes the use of linear functions implies the same assumptions of constant returns to scale and no input substitution which we discussed in the context of input-output models. In transportation models the use of linear functions usually implies that one has had to assume that people place similar value on each additional unit of time which they spend travelling. These sorts of assumptions may or may not be damaging and it is impossible to lay down hard and fast rules as to when they are acceptable. The decision must rest with the individual analyst.

We have used linear programming as one example of the sorts of techniques which are currently used by regional analysts. Many different types of model are available but most of them share with linear programming the characteristics of supplying a rather rigid framework and the ability to act as guides to decision making. None of them provide strictly accurate descriptions of the working of the socio-economic system but such strict descriptive faithfulness is in truth a rather unreasonable demand to make on any conceptualization. What we do have the right to ask of a conceptual model is that it seizes on the strategic relationships that control the phenomenon it describes and that it thereby permits us to manipulate and think freshly about the situation. We hope to have demonstrated that techniques like linear programming do encourage us to do this.

References 1 Introduction and perspective

Note: The works marked * would make good entry points into the literature *but only if you should want to read further after the course.* We need only add that one can choose to make a fresh approach to the topic through a book about regional geography like Minshull (1967), or an article like Kimble (1951). Or there are books about the regional concept like Dickinson (1947), and articles like Gilbert (1957). Or you may prefer to attack through books written as regional geography like Vidal de la Blache (1903) on France, Ogilvie (1928) on Britain, James (1959) on Latin America, or Spate and Learmonth (1967) on India and Pakistan, or in a somewhat more modern idiom Cole (1965) on Latin America or even Brookfield (1971) on Melanesia though the last-named would certainly claim that his book is about problems in a region rather than about a region as such. After teaching regional geography for many years, Professor Learmonth has long held that regional geography cannot really be taught, though it can be practised by the pupil. So your view of regional geography is likely to be the more positive and constructive, the nearer you get to doing your own regional geography vicariously through participating in the regional geographer's analyses and syntheses as you read his work, or personally through your own work in the field, library and cartographic and statistical laboratory. (Don't be alarmed, these can be at home!) Once again, though, we have to say that work of this scale inevitably lies beyond the scope of this course.

*BROOKFIELD, H. C. (1971) *Melanesia; a geographical interpretation of an island world*, London, Methuen.

*COLE, J. P. (1965) *Latin America*, London, Butterworths.

*DICKINSON, R. E. (1947) *City, Region and Regionalism*, London, Routledge and Kegan Paul.

DURY, G. H. (1963) *The British Isles; a Systematic and Regional Geography* (2nd edn.) London, Heinemann. A recommended text for the course (see Block 1, Part 1).

GILBERT, E. W. (1957) 'Geography and Regionalism', Chapter XV in G. Taylor (ed.) *Geography in the Twentieth Century*, (3rd edn.) London, Methuen.

ISARD, W. (1960) *Methods of Regional Analysis; an Introduction to Regional Science*, New York, MIT/Wiley.

*JAMES, P. E. (1959) *Latin America* (3rd edn.), London, Cassell.

*KIMBLE, G. H. T. (1952) 'The inadequacy of the regional concept', Chapter 9 in Stamp, L. D. and Wooldridge, S. W. (eds.) *London Essays in Geography*, London, Longmans.

LEARMONTH, A. T. A. (1964) 'Retrospect on a project in applied regional geography', pp. 323–48 in Steel, R. W. and Prothero, R. M. (eds.) *Geographers and the Tropics; Liverpool Essays*, London, Longmans.

*MINSHULL, R. (1967) *Regional Geography; theory and practice*, London, Hutchinson.

*SPATE, O. H. K. and LEARMONTH, A. T. A. (1967) *India and Pakistan; a General and Regional Geography* (3rd edn.), London, Methuen.

SOUTH EAST JOINT PLANNING TEAM (1970) *Strategic Plan for the South East*, London, HMSO.

THE OPEN UNIVERSITY (1970) 'Societies and Environments', D100 Social Science Foundation Course, *Understanding Society*, Unit 4, Bletchley, The Open University Press.

THE OPEN UNIVERSITY (1971) 'Evolution or revolution in geography', D281 Social Sciences: a second level course, *New trends in geography*, Block 1, Part 1 'Continuity and change', Part 2 'Geographic data and methods', Part 3 'Why has geography changed?'

*VIDAL DE LA BLACHE, P. (1911) *Tableau de la géographie de la France*, Paris, Hachette.

WRIGLEY, E. A. (1971) 'Changes in the philosophy of geography', Chapter 1, pp. 3–20, in Chorley, R. J. and Haggett, P. (eds.) *Frontiers in Geographical Teaching*, (2nd edn.) London, Methuen.

References   2   Aspects of Regional Analysis

FRIEDMANN, J. and ALONSO, W. (1964) *Regional Development and Planning; a reader*, Cambridge, Mass., M.I.T. Press. (Includes Tiebout, 'Exports and Regional Economic Growth'.)

ISARD, W. (1960) *Methods of Regional Analysis*, Cambridge, Mass., M.I.T. Press, New York, Wiley.

ISARD, W. *et al.* (1969) *General Theory; social, political, economic and regional, with particular reference to decision making analysis*, Cambridge, Mass., M.I.T. Press.

MIERNYK, W. H. (1965) *The Elements of Input-Output Analysis*, New York, Random House.

NEEDLEMAN, L. (1968) *Regional Analysis; selected readings*, London, Penguin. (Includes Tiebout, 'Regional and inter-regional input-output models; an appraisal'.)

New Trends in Geography